T0244182

Unraveling the Myth
of Sgt. Alvin York

C. A. Brannen Series

Unraveling the Myth of Sgt. Alvin York

THE OTHER SIXTEEN

James P. Gregory Jr.

Texas A&M University Press / College Station

∞ This paper meets the requirements of ANSI/NISO Z39.48–1992
(Permanence of Paper).
Binding materials have been chosen for durability.
Manufactured in the United States of America

Library of Congress Cataloging-in-Publication Data

Names: Gregory, James P., Jr., 1995– author.
Title: Unraveling the myth of Sgt. Alvin York: the other sixteen / James
    P. Gregory Jr.
Other titles: C.A. Brannen series.
Description: First edition. | College Station: Texas A&M University Press,
    [2023] | Series: C.A. Brannen series | Includes bibliographical
    references and index.
Identifiers: LCCN 2022034430 (print) | LCCN 2022034431 (ebook) | ISBN
    9781648430756 (hardcover) | ISBN 9781648430763 (ebook)
Subjects: LCSH: York, Alvin Cullum, 1887–1964—In mass media. | United
    States. Army. Division, 82nd—Biography. | Argonne, Battle of the,
    France, 1918—Biography. | World War, 1914–1918—Regimental
    histories—United States. | BISAC: HISTORY / Wars & Conflicts / World
    War I | HISTORY / United States / 20th Century | LCGFT: Biographies.
Classification: LCC D545.A63 G74 2023 (print) | LCC D545.A63 (ebook) |
    DDC 940.4/360922—dc23/eng/20220726
LC record available at https://lccn.loc.gov/2022034430
LC ebook record available at https://lccn.loc.gov/2022034431

To My Mother

Contents

Acknowledgments

Unraveling the Myth of Sgt. Alvin York is a culmination of over twelve years of research dedicated to finally demolishing the myth of Sgt. Alvin York and giving credit to the Other Sixteen who were part of his patrol as they fought the Germans that October day in 1918. I would first like to explain the story behind this work. In 2017, at Steven Girard's behest, I contacted Robert D'Angelo, the great-nephew of Bernard Early, to discuss their perspectives on the battle. For the first two years, the descendants were wary of opening their archives. Indeed, my initial research placed me firmly in the popular camp that saw Alvin York as the only hero of the battle. The other men of the patrol, it seemed, were merely guarding prisoners or were not participating at all. However, as I began digging into the subject my perception changed. The stories of the survivors had been given very little weight. They seemed to be frustrated with the lack of acknowledgment despite every attempt to bring their stories to the public.

As I read the secondary literature, I realized that those attempts had been used against the other survivors to make them seem greedy and jealous. Various authors used their perceived ill intentions to skew the story of the Other Sixteen. Instead of authors using all of the accounts together, they consistently followed York's perspective, citing the Medal of Honor investigation as the definitive research into the matter. Instead of researching the claims of the other survivors, authors simply wrote them off. Was it possible that out of eleven survivors, the story of just one of them held weight? This possibility did not sit right with me, and I felt that it deserved a deeper investigation.

After contacting the descendants, 100 years of history opened up to me and combined with my research to show a completely different story. The men were not jealous; nor were they greedy. They simply wanted to be acknowledged for their roles, combatting the York myth that it was a story of a "single-handed" capture. This work is dedicated to telling their stories the way they saw it. Some of their stories of the battle contain some contradictions, just as is expected from the fog of war. However, the facts can be pulled from the fog by looking at the survivors' recollections after the war. Such a large undertaking was possible only through the help of a multitude of individuals who worked to find every document that was available, whether they were obscure or history-breaking. With that said, I would like to express my sincerest gratitude to all of those who took part in this endeavor from both the foundation work for this book to its final edits.

First among those to whom I owe thanks are the descendants of the Other Sixteen, who deserve a hefty thank you for laying the foundation for my research. Robert V. D'Angelo Jr. started the original search for the truth and gathered together the descendants. His initial research and thousands of hours spent gathering material and tracking down relatives provided a remarkable wealth of information that I trust honors the memory of the Other Sixteen and their families. Robert's work proved to be priceless in establishing the most detailed version of this story possible. David Kornacki became the gatekeeper for the Other Sixteen website, which unfortunately is no longer available, and his work with Robert secured the future of the Other Sixteen's legacy. His work researching his grandfather's experience guided my research and proved to be very helpful in expanding the story. Jimmy Fallon became the caretaker of his grandfather's (Otis Merrithew) collection of documents dating from 1918 into the 1960s. It is safe to say that without access to these documents, the truth, after the passage of a whole century, would not have seen the light of day. I am indebted to him for sharing the wealth of knowledge found within that collection. The descendants of Patrick Donohue—Patricia Waters, Keith Waters, and Jeffrey Waters— all assisted in piecing together the story of Patrick. Their insight provided helpful information that finally give him a voice in his own story. Finally, to all the other descendants whom I did not name, your role in remembering, fighting for, and sharing your relative's story has finally come to fruition with this book. I hope that you take comfort in the fact that their stories will now be told and preserved for future generations.

The largest personal thank you belongs to Staff Sgt. Steven C. Girard, US Army (Ret.). As a very close friend and mentor in creating this work, I am truly in his debt. Without his continual enthusiasm, this book would not be where it is now. His passion for this story not only set the stage for this work but also saw it through to its end. Years of assistance in the research—talking me down when it seemed like this story was too complicated to be pieced back together and pushing me to dig deeper to make it the best possible version—need to be acknowledged. I also owe a large thank you to Brad Posey. Without his help, I would not have had access to the German archives, and this story would not have been as complete as it is. He translated the German documents, which were approved by a court-appointed translator. His deep knowledge of the battle site and the primary documentation was invaluable and helped make this story much more complete.

I owe much to those individuals who assisted me in finding the documents necessary to tell this story. Cynthia Johnson helped track down very obscure documents related to the story of Patrick Donohue, an endeavor that took several weeks for which I am truly grateful. Stephanie Aude also helped locate the final pieces after being contacted by Cynthia. I thank you both for your work. In the same context, Louise Sandberg from the Lawrence Public Library provided me with several local articles about Donohue. Scott Schoner also spent several hours tracking down records for this book, for which I am deeply grateful.

Some individuals may not realize how important their contribution truly was to this, work. Sgt. Maj. Hubert Caloud, US Marine Corps (Ret.), of the American Battle Monuments Commission, provided access to some of the most important documents for this book. Thank you for assisting in this endeavor. Mike Cunha, the creator of the *Battles of the First World War* podcast, provided the first platform to share the story of the Other Sixteen. Thank you for allowing me to share the story of these forgotten men.

The people who perhaps do not get enough credit in books are those friends who served as editors. They read through many drafts of this book and graciously provided their valuable time to tear apart the early iterations of this book. For this effort, I am very grateful and owe them more than just a thank you. Madeline Johnson read through many drafts of this work. Her brutal honesty and insightful comments greatly influenced my writing. Thank you for spending so much of your valuable time to assist me in creating this book. Dr. Mark Janzen edited this work to ensure that it upheld a high academic standard. I also owe thanks to Alexander Barnes for editing early drafts of the work.

I would also like to acknowledge and thank the friends who listened to me talk about this research ad nauseum: notably, Landon Coulter,

Logan Ray, Matthew Hill, Adam Krejčí, and Winn Carroll, the last of whom promised to assign this book in his classes. Finally, I owe thanks to my family who supported me throughout this work and graciously listened to me tell this story to them countless times. Your constant support helped me throughout this endeavor. I love and thank you all. I also want to express my deepest gratitude to my grandfather, George Gregory, who supported me throughout this project but did not get to see its completion. I hope this work would have made him proud.

Unraveling the Myth
of Sgt. Alvin York

Prologue

My journey into World War I American Expeditionary Forces (AEF) history began many years ago as a small child who listened to the stories of my family members who served as Marines in France with the 4th Brigade (Marine), 2nd Division, AEF. They fought in some of the most famous battles of World War I from Belleau Wood to the Meuse-Argonne Offensive.

Growing up with World War I veterans and hearing their stories inspired me to enlist in the US Army in the mid-1980s, where I was later assigned as a US Army Unit Historical Officer. After retiring, I dedicated myself to helping families uncover the histories of their relatives who had fought in the war as a way to honor those men and their sacrifices. I also dedicated myself to researching the war, especially the Marine Corps and the Second Division, AEF. During my research, one event always struck me as odd: the story of Sgt. Alvin York and the battle of Chatel-Chéhéry, France, on the morning of Tuesday, October 8, 1918.

The popular story claimed that Sgt. York had almost singlehandedly knocked out 35 enemy machine guns, captured 132 German soldiers, and killed 25 Germans after the other noncommissioned officers had been knocked out of action. It was a hard story to believe. As a combat veteran myself, I understood the tunnel vision and chaos of a firefight. It is hard to know what others are doing during the fight because you are focused on keeping yourself alive and eliminating the threat. It was not until several years ago, when I came across a video of the descendants of the "Other Sixteen" who argued for their relatives' participation in the battle that made Sgt. Alvin York famous, that I finally saw that there was truly more to the story.

Previously, I had worked with James Gregory on his first three books and knew that he would be the perfect person to take a fresh new look at the story of Alvin York. After I contacted James in September 2018, he made contact with the descendants of the "Other Sixteen" and expressed his desire to write a book using their perspectives and story. A few months later, I accompanied James on a trip to meet with Robert D'Angelo and Dave Kornacki, descendants of two of the "Other Sixteen," Bernard Early and Joseph Kornacki. James showed these descendants that he had the capability and energy to tackle this project.

James has taken the story above and beyond the expectations of the descendants and has revealed a fascinating tale of myth making, cover-ups, deceit, and redemption. The narrative that you are about to read will shed new light on aspects of this subject that have never been fully discussed or acknowledged by any author who has covered the history of the AEF during World War I. James Gregory finally reveals the truth behind Sgt. Alvin C. York and the "Other Sixteen" from Chatel-Chéhéry to the present. I am proud to have worked with him on this project and to have contributed to preserving the memory of these brave heroes. Lastly, to the "Other Sixteen" and their descendants, you are not forgotten, and through this work we believe an injustice will finally be righted.

Staff Sgt. Steven C. Girard, US Army (Ret.)
Unit Historical Officer, US Army

Introduction

The York Myth

On the morning of October 8, 1918, the left flank of the 82nd Division was raked with German machine gun fire on the left, right, and front. The progress of Company G along the left side of the advance stalled due to the heavy fire. 2nd Lt. Kirby Stewart was leading his men at the front of the line when a burst of enemy machine gun fire cut him down. Command fell to Sgt. Harry Parsons who detailed a patrol of seventeen men, led by Acting Sgt. Bernard Early to undertake a mission to silence the German machine guns. This patrol consisted of Acting Sgt. Bernard Early, Cpl. Murray Savage, Acting Cpl. Alvin C. York, Acting Cpl. Otis Merrithew [William Cutting], and Pvts. Carl Swanson, Feodor Sok, Fred Wareing, George Wills, Joseph Kornacki, Mario Muzzi, Maryan Dymowski, Michael Sacina, Patrick Donohue, Percy Beardsley, Ralph Weiler, Thomas Johnson, and William Wine.

The men followed Early as he led them through the dense forest and brush seeking to avoid the eyes of the German machine gun nests up on the hillside. A morning mist helped to hide the patrol as they crossed the valley. When they reached the base of the hill, the men jumped into an old German trench and followed it up and over the hill to reach the other side where they continued moving stealthily through the forest. As they walked into a wooded ravine, they could hear the drum of heavy machine gun fire from the ridge above them. Finally, the Americans halted at a stream where they did not have as much cover.

Suddenly, Murray Savage called out as two Germans wearing Red Cross armbands darted from the brush near the stream. The Americans yelled at them to stop and then fired, missing both. The Germans rushed North along the stream back to their unit with the Americans chasing close behind. Early broke his men into several smaller groups and pushed into the brush after the Germans.

The patrol abruptly found themselves face to face with a German unit of around one hundred men having breakfast. The Germans were resting with their weapons stacked near them while a German commander spoke. They were completely unprepared for a fight. The Americans opened fire, causing chaos amongst the Germans who immediately attempted to surrender. Early ordered his men to cease fire and moved in to capture the Germans.

The Americans stripped the Germans of their weapons and equipment. They lined them up in two rows and prepared to march them back to the American lines. Suddenly, a German command rang out and the prisoners hit the ground. The confused Americans were then cut down by rifle and machine gun fire from a group of Germans previously unnoticed lying on the hillside above them. Six Americans were instantly killed. Cpl. Savage, Pvt. Dymowski, Pvt. Swanson, Pvt. Wareing, Pvt. Weiler, and Pvt. Wine were all killed almost instantly in the fire.

Three others were severely wounded and taken out of the action. Acting Sgt. Early, Acting Cpl. Merrithew, and Pvt. Muzzi were incapacitated. This left Acting Cpl. Alvin York as the last noncommissioned officer standing. While the other men of the patrol found cover in the brush or around the German prisoners, York crawled up the hill to get a better vantage point.

York found cover against a tree as bullets rained around him. York, a renowned marksman back home in Tennessee, picked off the Germans on the hill one by one. Due to his position, the Germans had to peek over to see him and therefore became easy targets for this sharpshooter. The Germans could not hit him. Not even the German major who had already been taken prisoner but fired at York with his pistol. York was untouchable and kept the German's heads down. He fired so much, that York began to run out of ammunition in the front pouches of his ammunition belt.

A few of the other Americans in the patrol attempted to keep up fire against the Germans. Pvt. Beardsley fired with his pistol while a few others fired a few shots with their rifles. However, their role was small, while York took the brunt of the initiative in the fight. Out of the corner of his eye, York spotted a German officer who charged at him with several other soldiers. York had already emptied all the rounds for his rifle and switched to his .45 automatic pistol.

As the Germans charged at him, York thought back to the turkey shoots he used to participate in while living in Tennessee. To keep the turkeys from scattering, he would shoot the one in the back first and then move forward. He saw this as his best method to exterminate this threat of charging Germans. He coolly aimed down his sights and shot each German until finally shooting the officer in the stomach who fell to the ground, screaming in agony.

Due to his deadly shooting, the German Major, who had been previously captured with the initial group, called out to York. He told York that if he would stop shooting, he would make the rest of the Germans surrender. York agreed and the commander blew his whistle as a signal for the others to come down from the hillside. As the Germans came down from their positions, one threw a grenade at York, but it missed. York quickly dispatched the man. In all, York now had over 100 prisoners, but he had to get them back to the American lines.

York ordered the remaining American survivors to line up the prisoners and assigned a few prisoners to assist the wounded Early. To ensure no more issues, York forced the German major to march at the front of the column with York's pistol stuck to his back. As they marched, the major would force other Germans to surrender to the group. As they were preparing to begin marching out of the woods, another German officer and a group of his men rushed out of the woods, with their bayonets. However, upon seeing the German major and the other prisoners, they stopped in their tracks. The major ordered them to surrender and told him that he would take responsibility. So the number of prisoners grew.

York decided to march the prisoners out towards the other machine guns and forced the German major to have the other machine gun nests surrender. As they returned back to the American lines, an artillery barrage forced the column to make double time. Fortunately, York and his group soon ran into their own unit, Company G, who had been pushing forward all morning. Upon seeing this mass of prisoners 1st Lt. Joseph Woods counted York's prisoners to find they had captured 132.

Lt. Woods gave York more men to help guard the prisoners and ordered him to take them back to headquarters in Varennes. Acting Sgt. Early, Acting Cpl. Merrithew, Pvt. Muzzi, and Pvt. Donohue were evacuated in ambulances as the column continued on. Upon arriving in Varennes, Brig. Gen. Julian R. Lindsey said to York, "I hear you have captured the whole damn Germany army." To which York responded that he only had 132.[1]

This is the myth of Alvin York. It is a combination of several different versions of York's legend that evolved in order to fit the narrative of individuals outside of the patrol. Many aspects of this story were exaggerated or left out as the story changed hands. The battle grew from a shared experience of seventeen men into a tale of a single man fighting practically unassisted and capturing 132 Germans. This book tells the story of the other sixteen men in the patrol and puts their perspectives of the battle in the proper place alongside York.

To give the men their due and to set the story straight, *Unraveling the Myth of Sgt. Alvin York* has reconstructed their actions before and after the October 8, 1918, engagement. This book is based on documents and letters never made public before, official government archival sources recently opened, and interviews with the descendants of the survivors. This new material reveals the cover-ups, slander, and public misconceptions that arose when other parties, who were not present at the battle, used Alvin York's story to further their own agendas.

Unraveling the Myth of Sgt. Alvin York is written with the goal of presenting a balanced history of Sgt. Alvin York. The legend and myth have created a story that is devoid of the other patrol members. The survivors have been described as jealous and bitter men who wanted something they did not deserve. However, they were victims, just as York was, of outside sources who wanted to capitalize on their shared story. So what does the story look like if the preconceived notions of intent are dropped, German primary documents are taken into account, and the stories of the other men are given equal weight? By bringing these sources into account, a more historically balanced story is revealed.

1

Origins, The Other Sixteen

The myth of Sgt. Alvin York evolved over one hundred years as various people and organizations promoted it for their own advantage. These groups added to and removed pieces until the 1941 Warner Bros. movie *Sergeant York* essentially cemented the myth in its current form. Historians have continued to reinforce this version of the story well into the twenty-first century. One essential piece of the story has been ignored and excluded from the narrative. This is the role of the other sixteen men in the patrol. Their attempts to address the idea of York being "single-handed" have routinely been left out of the story. The goal of this book is to tell their story and integrate their perspectives into the narrative where they can take their rightful place alongside Alvin York.

On the fateful morning of October 8, 1918, the patrol of seventeen men from very diverse backgrounds found themselves in a baptism of fire that would influence the rest of their lives. On the patrol were seven immigrants—two Irish, two Italians, three Polish—who had come to the United States to find a better life along with ten American citizens. This group of strangers, unlikely to have crossed paths back in the United States, found themselves joined together and outnumbered by the enemy eight to one.

Cpl. (Acting Sgt.) Bernard Early was born in Mohill, Ireland, on November 15, 1892. He emigrated to the United States in 1911. When he was inducted into the US Army in 1917, he lived in New Haven, Connecticut. His sister operated a boarding home on Franklin Street where he lived with his two other brothers, James and John. He worked as a rifle tester at the Winchester Repeating Arms Company and as a bartender in New Haven.[1]

Bernard Early.
Courtesy of Robert
D'Angelo.

Murray Savage.
Courtesy of Robert
D'Angelo.

Alvin York.
Courtesy of Robert
D'Angelo.

Cpl. Murray L. Savage was born in Richmond, New York, on October 27, 1892. He worked on a farm in Bristol, New York, when he was inducted into the US Army on September 27, 1917, at Canandaigua, New York. Savage was originally part of Battery E, 2nd Battalion, 307th US Field Artillery Regiment, 153rd Field Artillery Brigade, 78th Division, American Expeditionary Forces (AEF) until November 14, 1917, when he transferred to Company G, 328th Regiment.[2] He would be killed in action on October 8, 1918, and is buried at Meuse-Argonne American Cemetery, Romagne-sous-Montfaucon, France. His mother, Elizabeth Savage, requested that his body remain in France, saying he should "lie in peace enveloped by the soil for which he gave his life. It was God's will that he should fall there, and it is my desire that he lay where he fell—with his brothers."[3] She later made the pilgrimage to visit his grave with the Gold Star Mothers in 1930.[4] Savage is still remembered in the Bloomfield Savage Post of the American Legion in Bloomfield, New York.

Pvt. First Class (Acting Cpl.) Alvin Cullum York was born in Pall Mall, Tennessee, on December 13, 1887. Growing up, he lived the simple life of a frontier family with little formal education. This life in the woods of Tennessee made York a sharpshooter from years of hunting, which translated well to his service in the US Army. York drank heavily and was a well-known "hellraiser" in his community until a religious conversion in 1914, after his friend Everret Delk was killed in a bar fight. York then devoted himself to the Church of Christ in Christian Union. When World War I broke out, York sought exemption from the draft several times as a conscientious objector but did not receive it. He joined Company G,

Otis Merrithew.
Courtesy of Robert
D'Angelo.

Carl Swanson.
*Soldiers of the Great War
Vol 2* (1920).

2nd Battalion, 328th Infantry, 82nd Division, AEF, and remained in the unit until the end of the war.[5]

Pvt. (Acting Cpl.) Otis Bernard Merrithew (William B. Cutting) was born in Boston, Massachusetts, on May 26, 1896. After his father abandoned the family, Otis dropped out of school to support his mother and four siblings. When the United States declared war, his mother did not want him to enlist or register for the draft. Otis registered anyway, but to do so he took the alias William B. Cutting, which he had seen on a storefront in North Adams, Massachusetts. At the time he was inducted into the US Army on October 4, 1917, at Bridgeport, Connecticut, Merrithew worked as an iceman for the Naugatuck Valley Ice Company. Originally assigned to Company K, 3rd Battalion, 304th Regiment, 152nd Brigade, 76th Division, AEF, Merrithew was later transferred to Company G, 328th Regiment. His brother George also fought in the war and was lost at sea while serving aboard the battleship USS *Nebraska*. In the original documents relating to his service, Merrithew is referred to by his alias William Cutting. This book will use his real name, Otis Merrithew.[6]

Pvt. Carl Frederick Swanson was born in Spring Creek Township, Pennsylvania, on April 3, 1896. His father, Amandus, was killed in 1905 in an accident at the tannery where he worked. In 1913, the family moved to Jamestown, New York, to seek better opportunities.[7] Carl worked at the Art Metal Construction Company as a press hand when he was inducted into the US Army on September 27, 1917. He was originally assigned to Battery C, 2nd Battalion, 307th US Field Artillery, 153rd Field Artillery Brigade, 76th Division, AEF, until November 14,

Fred Wareing.
Soldiers of the Great War Vol 2 (1920).

George Wills.
The Bristol Herald Courier,
November 11, 1929.

Mario Muzzi.
The Bristol Herald Courier,
November 11, 1929.

1917, when he transferred to Company G, 328th Infantry Regiment. Swanson was killed in action on October 8, 1918, and his body was later returned to the United States to be interred at Lake View Cemetery, Jamestown, New York.[8]

Pvt, Feodor Sok was born in Russia on April 25, 1894, and emigrated to the United States on May 21, 1914. He worked as a laborer for George Lamb & Sons in Buffalo, New York, when he was inducted into the US Army on September 29, 1917. He was originally assigned to Company A, 1st Battalion, 309th Infantry Regiment, 155th Brigade, 78th Division, AEF, until November 11, 1917, when he transferred to Regimental Head-quarters Company, 328th Infantry Regiment. He was later transferred to Company G on March 21, 1918.[9]

Pvt, Nedwell "Fred" Wareing was born in Lonsdale, Rhode Island, on October 19, 1894. He was living in New Bedford, Massachusetts, when he was inducted into the US Army in 1917. Fred was killed in action on October 8, 1918, and is buried at Meuse-Argonne American Cemetery, Romagne-sous-Montfaucon, France.[10] His mother, Flora, made the pilgrimage to visit his grave with the Gold Star Mothers in 1930.[11] On the night before she learned her son had been killed in action, Flora said she had dreamed that Fred appeared in uniform to tell her, "It's alright, Ma."[12]

Pvt. George Washington Wills was born in Philadelphia, Pennsylvania, on February 17, 1896. He worked as a machinist at the Pennsylvania Salt Works when he was inducted into the US Army on September 22, 1917.[13]

Pvt. Joseph S. Kornacki (Konotski) was born on August 15, 1895, in Warsaw, Poland. He emigrated to the United States with his father and

Joseph Kornacki and his family. Courtesy of David Kornacki.

brother in 1909. In 1910, Kornacki boarded in Hatfield, Massachusetts, as a farm laborer. He later moved to Holyoke, Massachusetts, where he worked as a paper maker at the American Writing Paper Co. when he was inducted into the US Army on October 7, 1917. The original documents pertaining to his service spell his last name phonetically as Konotski; however, in this book, it will be spelled correctly as Kornacki.[14]

Pvt. Mario Muzzi was born on October 8, 1888, in Civita di Bagnoregio, Italy.[15] He immigrated to the United States on November 19, 1910, and settled in New York City. He worked as a baker at the National Biscuit Co. in New York City when he was inducted into the US Army on September 29, 1917. Muzzi was originally assigned to 16th Company, 152nd Depot Brigade until transferring to Company C, 320th Machine Gun Battalion, 163rd Brigade, 82nd Division, AEF, on October 29, 1917. He was later transferred to Company G on April 6, 1918.[16]

Pvt. Maryan Edward Dymowski was born in Plock, Poland, on March 24, 1890. He immigrated to the United States on October 28, 1906, arriving with his mother, brother, and sister.[17] He worked as an assembler at the Bridgeport Brass Co. in Bridgeport, Connecticut, when he was inducted into the US Army in 1917. He was killed in action on October 8, 1918, and is buried at Meuse-Argonne American Cemetery, Romagne-sous-Montfaucon, France. His mother made the pilgrimage to visit his grave with the Gold Star Mothers in 1930.[18]

Pvt. Michael Angelo Sacina was born on July 25, 1888, in Rapone, Italy. He immigrated to the United States in 1906 and became a naturalized citizen in 1908. For a time, he lived with his brothers, Joseph and Frank, on St. Anne's Avenue in the Bronx, New York City. He worked at a wire spring factory when he was inducted into the US Army on September 22, 1917.[19]

Pvt. Patrick J. Donohue was born in Cork, Ireland, on January 8, 1888. He immigrated to the United States in 1905. At the outbreak of the war, he was attending night school and worked as a mill worker at the Arlington Mill in Lawrence, Massachusetts. He was inducted into the US Army on October 5, 1917.[20]

Pvt. Percy Peck Beardsley was born in Roxbury, Connecticut, on August 6, 1891. He grew up and worked as the superintendent on his family's farm where they raised Devonshire cattle. He spent his spare time hunting in the woods around his home which, like York, also translated to his skills in the army. He was inducted into the US Army on October 3, 1917.[21]

Maryan Dymowski.
Courtesy of Carol
Schulthies.

Michael Sacina.
*The Bristol Herald
Courier*, November 11,
1929.

Patrick Donohue.
The Evening Tribune,
November 29, 1941.

Percy Beardsley.
Connecticut WWI Military
Questionnaires, 1919–1920.
Connecticut State Library.

Ralph Weiler.
*York County and the World
War, 1914–1919* (1920).

William Wine.
*Soldiers of the Great War,
Vol. 3* (1920).

Pvt. Ralph Eugene Weiler was born in Hanover, Pennsylvania, on October 16, 1895. He worked as a laborer when he was inducted into the US Army on September 19, 1917. Weiler was originally assigned to Company H, 316th Infantry, 158th Brigade, 79th Division, until transferring to Company G, 328th Infantry, 82nd Division, on October 18, 1917. His brother, Raymond Weiler, was also inducted that day and served in the 301st Field Bakery Co. Service of Supply, AEF. Ralph was killed in action on October 8, 1918, and is buried in the Meuse-Argonne American Cemetery, Romagne-sous-Montfaucon, France. He was the first member of the Minnewaukaru tribe to be killed in World War I.[22] His mother, Louise, made the pilgrimage to visit his grave with the Gold Star Mothers in 1930.[23]

Pvt. Thomas Gibbs Johnson was born in Lynchburg, Virginia, on June 5, 1895. When he registered for the draft, he described himself as a student in Lynchburg. He was inducted into the US Army on June 1918. Johnson was a replacement and therefore joined Company G later in the war. Johnson traveled to France with the 40th Provisional Company August Infantry Replacement Draft aboard the USS *Martha Washington* on August 14, 1918.[24]

Pvt. William Edward Wine was born in Philadelphia, Pennsylvania, on February 4, 1896. He was working as a machine operator in the Frankford Arsenal when he was inducted into the US Army.[25] He was killed in action on October 8, 1918, and is buried in the Meuse-Argonne American Cemetery, Romagne-sous-Montfaucon, France.

When the dust settled after the battle, six members of the patrol lay dead and four were wounded. Despite these sacrifices, one man soon became the focal point of the battle. Alvin York would become the "greatest hero of World War I," being credited with capturing, single-handedly, 132 German prisoners, knocking out many machine gun nests, and killing over twenty-five Germans near Chatel-Chéhéry, France, on October 8, 1918, during the Meuse-Argonne Offensive. York would be promoted to the rank of sergeant. He would be decorated with the Medal of Honor, the French Legion of Honor, French Military Medal, French 1914–1918 Croix de Guerre with Palm, Italian War Merit Cross, and the Order of Prince Danilo I from Montenegro. When he returned to the United States, he was celebrated as a hero and received even more honors and praise. Magazines, books, and journals told the story of his single-handed prowess.

But how did this legend evolve? And how could it come to exclude the actions of sixteen other men?

It originated soon after the armistice took effect on November 11, 1918, with Sgt. York's exploits at Chatel-Chéhéry spreading by word of mouth (this rise in popularity will be discussed in more detail in chapter three). As his story spread through the 82nd Division, it inspired Chaplain (Capt.) John P. Tyler to take Sgt. York on a six-week tour of France to raise morale by telling his story.[26]

York's tale attracted the interest of his commanding officers, especially Maj. Gen. George B. Duncan, Commanding General of the 82nd Division, AEF. Sandra S. Turner, a graduate of the Alvin C. York Agricultural Institute, has argued that Maj. Gen. Duncan became, in a sense, York's first press agent. Duncan saw York's story as an opportunity to further his own reputation. Duncan began describing York's feat as a single-handed fight. In fact, in his postwar memoir, *Reminiscences of the World War*, Duncan discussed York and said outright that "his fight was single handed."[27] Duncan first gave the story about York to the American press while sitting for the American portrait artist, Joseph Cummings Chase, who had been commissioned to paint American Distinguished Service Cross recipients during and after the war.[28] During a session, Duncan had regaled Chase with the story of York as a conscientious objector who turned warrior. Soon after, Chase met York to paint his portrait. After their meeting, Chase wrote his own brief article on York in *World's Work* in April 1919.[29] However, Chase's story would not receive nearly as much attention as the article by George Pattullo that came out in the *Saturday Evening Post*, also in April 1919.

In late January of 1919, the 82nd Division headquarters contacted *Saturday Evening Post* war correspondent George Pattullo with the suggestion that he write an article about Sgt. York at Chatel-Chéhéry. On January 26, Pattullo responded that he "would be glad to undertake story of corporal York if it is withheld from newspapers."[30] Pattullo wanted to ensure that he would be the only one to cover this story.

Pattullo made his way to France from Koblenz, Germany, where he was covering the US Third Army of Occupation. At the time, American war correspondents needed riveting material that would make it past the censors. The famous muckraking journalist, George Seldes, characterized several of the correspondents he knew while serving in the United States Press Corps during World War I as having "no social conscience . . . and not even a social thought. So far as I know, no one cared a damn about anything at all except getting the news, preferably getting it first, and not necessarily getting it objectively or too truthfully."[31]

Pattullo would use York's story to further his own career as a writer. Pattullo traveled to Prauthoy, France, where he was invited to join the official investigating team that was conducting the Medal of Honor investigation at the engagement area near Chatel-Chéhéry on February 7, 1919. George Pattullo called his version of York's story, which was based on the investigation, "The Second Elder Gives Battle," and it appeared in the *Saturday Evening Post* on April 26, 1919. The title of the article referred to York's position at his church. Pattullo highlighted York's faith, saying that "because of the man's deep religious convictions and scruples" his accomplishment stood as the "greatest individual feat of the war."[32]

Pattullo's religion-centric approach reflected a blend of Christianity and patriotism that sociologist Robert Bellah has labeled the American civil religion, where God is manifest in history and Americans are his chosen people. Bellah characterized this religion as "not the worship of the American nation but an understanding of the American experience in the light of ultimate and universal reality."[33] The reason York could perform his feat "single-handedly" is because God was protecting him. Alvin York was the Lord's agent in the Argonne Forest.[34]

Pattullo's *Saturday Evening Post* article, which would be the origin story of the popular York myth, put the other sixteen men in the background. Although Pattullo mentions their names, in his version they are relegated to guarding prisoners or, in the case of Percy Beardsley, unable to do anything.[35] Pattullo also claimed that during the fight some Germans charged at York, but York shot their lieutenant in the front first, then killed the others. Pattullo presents York as the ideal American soldier and human being with no faults. Pattullo's portrait of York as a religious hero serving with the Lord's favor, gave his story the consideration of truth even at the expense of the other sixteen. To question York would be to question God's power.

Pattullo's article was intended for mass civilian circulation, but Lt. Col. G. Edward Buxton Jr. would use the *Official History of 82nd Division American Expeditionary Forces,* published in 1919, to present the military side of the story. Buxton's account of the battle is also based on the Medal of Honor investigation and statements from four survivors: Percy Beardsley, Michael Sacina, George Wills, and Patrick Donohue. Buxton reports that Acting Sgt. Bernard Early led the group of seventeen men and captured "a large body of Germans surrounding the German battalion commander." Buxton then devoted a page to York's version of the battle and says York took "the chief burden of initiative and achievement" while "a few shots were fired by the remaining three Americans."[36] Buxton also mentions that Germans charged at York during the fight, but he repeated Pattullo's description of the event. Although Buxton later changed his views on the battle, his account reinforced the idea that the other men were either casualties or noncontributors in the engagement.

In the 1920s, two authors approached York to write his story. The first, Samuel K. Cowan, another native of Tennessee, published the first book on York, titled *Sergeant York and His People,* in 1922. Cowan focused on York's life in Appalachia rather than his military service. Cowan attempted to understand the environment that created Alvin York and his views. Cowan devoted a chapter to the 1918 battle but repeated the same story as that of the previous authors, with the exception that the "charging" Germans crept toward York rather than appearing from a trench. It was Cowan who created the detail of the "turkey shoot," which would become a central feature of the York myth. Cowan reported that York shot the charging Germans one by one, moving from the back to front, just as he had supposedly learned to shoot turkeys back in Tennessee.[37] At the end of the book, Cowan provides the affidavits from Patrick Donohue, Michael Sacina, Percy Beardsley, and George Wills to showcase York's actions. Cowan used these statements to reinforce the "single-handed" claim, saying that "in the height of the fight, not a shot was fired but by York."[38] The book's reviews were unenthusiastic, and it achieved only limited circulation, garnering only 300 advance orders.[39]

In 1928, Thomas J. Skeyhill published *Sergeant York: His Own Life Story and War Diary.* Skeyhill's book became—and still is—the main source of the information that upholds the myth of Sgt. Alvin York. Skeyhill based his version of York's story on his war diary and records of the War Department. Unfortunately, most of the simple annotations in York's diary were made during the war along with considerable false information added by York after the war. Skeyhill's version left out some of these notes, including the claim "I never was a conscientious objector."[40] While excluding some sections, Skeyhill bolstered his claims in the book by publishing the original affidavits provided for York's Medal of Honor investigation as well as affidavits procured from Bernard Early and Harry Parsons.[41] Skeyhill included details about the personalities and backgrounds of many of the other sixteen. However, it is difficult to know if these descriptions came from York or if Skeyhill created them to make a better story. Skeyhill had a history of deception, and his work on York's story contained "questionable history of the type he had made a career of pedaling."[42] When discussing the battle, Skeyhill listed the other men of the patrol but did not give them any role in the fighting. Instead, Skeyhill claims that some of the men huddled with the prisoners while others moved to cover. According to him, they did not actively participate in the battle.[43] Skeyhill, like Cowan, tailored York's story to fit his narrative.

Historian David D. Lee points out that Skeyhill wrote most of his biography as if York himself were telling the story in the first person. Skeyhill modified York's accent so that it would be a folksy mountain dialect. Cowan and Skeyhill created a myth of Alvin York with no faults worth mentioning. The perception that these two authors, most prominently Skeyhill, created had a deep influence on the public viewpoint that continues to this day.[44] Both authors are also responsible for the practice of not using Otis Merrithew's real name and referring to him with the alias he served under, William Cutting. Alvin York had learned of Merrithew's true identity in 1920, during a speaking engagement in Boston.[45] However, he must not have revealed this to the authors who referred to Merrithew only as Cutting.

In 1930, Skeyhill also published *Sergeant York: Last of the Long Hunters* as a rewritten version for the juvenile market. He rewrote York's story as a frontier adventure with fewer facts and more stories about the mountain man turned soldier. Because it was directed to children, it exposed generations to a myth instead of York's actual story. Regarding the other sixteen men, at the beginning of the book Skeyhill stated that, although Bernard Early was leading the group, he turned command over to York: "You are a woodsman and a hunter, lead us to those machine guns." In regard to Merrithew, Skeyhill claimed that "although pretty nearly shot to pieces in the fight with the machine guns, he walked out with the slightly wounded cases. When Parsons greeted him . . . he was weak from loss of blood and vomiting with pain." Skeyhill also referred to Carl Swanson as "Walter Swanson."[46]

This book gives York all of the credit for the fighting. For example, the chapter about the battle is entitled "America's One-Man Army."[47] Instead of York's version, which included "seven other soldiers," Skeyhill emphasized the myth that York single-handedly defeated and captured the Germans.[48] By giving so little attention to the roles of the other men in his books, Skeyhill would cement the myth in the public's imagination so firmly that through the years even official government action could not change the narrative. Historian David Lee called Samuel Cowan and Thomas Skeyhill "legend makers" who sacrificed the truth about York to make him a symbol of national values.[49] Several later authors and historians took the same approach when writing about York.

It was Sgt. Alvin York who began spreading his story, since he had indeed done a big part of the fighting on October 8, 1918. However, he would eventually become the victim of other parties who were interested in promoting and adjusting his story for their own advantage. They did this by adding and changing various aspects of the story. Maj. Gen. George Duncan attached himself to the myth, which he used to burnish his reputation as a commander. George Pattullo, Samuel Cowan, and Thomas Skeyhill built upon each other and became the foundational myth for twenty years until Warner Bros. would adjust and cement their version in popular culture.

Despite the modifications made by interested parties, the "single-handed" idea continued to gain traction, thereby diminishing the efforts and participation of the other sixteen members of the patrol. Like York, they would become victims of manipulation by outside parties. The survivors of the engagement, understandably, blamed York for their exclusion. It is, however, likely that York found himself under pressure from commanding officers, which he could not control.

The other survivors, in their own way, also suffered from the outside influences manipulating their shared experience. In response, after the war the survivors began to seek recognition for their roles in order to fight the "single-handed" myth. But to explain their later attempts, we need to step back to their entry into World War I.

2

Origins, Company G

The story of these men did not begin on October 8, 1918. By then, most of them had been in the army for over a year and had combat experience. The *History of the Three Hundred and Twenty-Eighth Regiment of Infantry, Eighty-Second Division*, tells the story of Company G of the 2nd Battalion, until that fateful date.[1]

The 82nd Division, AEF, was formed in the summer of 1917 at Camp Gordon, Georgia. While all the division's senior leaders were Regular Army officers, most of the junior officers were recent graduates of one of the Officers' Training Camps for civilians entering the Army. Many of the new officers were southerners, mostly from the state of Georgia. All the National Army Divisions, made up of draftees, were drawn from neighboring states and had a regional flavor. The initial plan for the 82nd was to make it up entirely of men from the southern states. On September 5, 1917, the first draftees began to arrive at Camp Gordon from Alabama, Georgia, and Tennessee. However, in October, these men transferred to fill the National Guard organizations. By October 20, each company of the 82nd Division had only its officers. New draftees from various northern and eastern camps soon arrived to fill the ranks. Soldiers representing western and midwestern states eventually joined as well. As a nod to the division's eclectic mixture of soldiers from throughout the United States, the 82nd Division adopted the nickname "All-American." They continued their training at Camp Gordon. Many were of foreign birth and not always able to read English or in some cases even speak it. However, "they were willing and anxious to learn and did so with surprising quickness."[2]

To remedy the language problem, the camp organized a system of company schools to teach the English language as well as other schools for intensive military training taught by British and French instructors. The men soon became proficient in not only English but also in the rifle, hand grenade, rifle grenade, bayonet, gas defense, and sniping. During their time at the camp, the men underwent intensive practical training in the uses of various arms and equipment by engaging in elaborate bayonet and grenade courses. Small-arms training occurred at an enormous rifle range at Norcross, Georgia. The range was located several miles away from the camp, so the men spent days at a time doing nothing but shooting. The men also learned from French engineers how to dig trench systems and build barbed wire entanglements. Finally, the men received gas mask instruction and had to pass through the gas house, which simulated battlefield exposure to poison gas.

The Division received its entraining orders and on April 1918 moved to Camp Upton, New York. On April 30, the men of Company G entrained to Boston Harbor where they would board the H.M.S *Scandinavian* to sail to New York. There a convoy of ships assembled, consisting of sixteen transports and one cruiser, the USS *San Diego*. The convoy departed for Liverpool, England, during the afternoon of May 3, 1918. They had an uneventful trip across the Atlantic Ocean. Being on a British ship, the men learned about British sea rations and crews, neither of which they found agreeable. They spent their time on board with physical exercise and boat drills. Bernard Early and Carl Swanson both appear to have missed their ship due to extended trips to say goodbye to their families. Early sailed on the SS *City of Brisbane* on May 7, and Swanson aboard SS *Themistocles* on May 11.[3] Upon arriving in England, they quickly rejoined their units.

The men arrived at Liverpool thirteen days later on May 16 and spent the entire day unloading the ships. They then marched to Knotty Ash Rest Camp on the outskirts of Liverpool. There they became acquainted with the British Army ration and, although they appreciated the jam, the average American soldier reportedly did not like the change from beef and coffee to cheese and tea. On May 18, the men entrained for the Southampton Rest Camp. During their stay at Southampton, they received a letter of welcome from King George V. The men also noted that the citizens, "especially the women, seemed greatly interested in us and did everything possible to add to our pleasure and enjoyment."[4]

On May 20, the men sailed to Le Havre, France, where they swapped their American rifles and bayonets for British equipment. They were to be deployed with the British 66th Division. The men of Company G received their steel helmets and gas masks with more training. The rest camps did not provide much rest as the men soon learned. At the camps in the vicinity of Le Havre, they slept on the floor with twenty-five men crowded into a small tent.

By May 23, the 328th Regiment had entrained at Le Havre for the town of Eu, about 40 miles behind the Somme front. The men then marched to their assigned areas near Abbeville, where they billeted in French barns and learned to pile enough hay to make a comfortable bed. There they began to familiarize themselves with lice or "cooties." In their reserve position on the Somme front, they could hear the roar of the artillery and had frequent visits from German planes. The town and surrounding countryside received heavy bombing almost every night, but the regiment had only one man slightly wounded.

Around June 1, the 328th Regiment marched to a new area near Elincourt. They continued their training schedule, quickly making them experts with the Lewis gun and British Lee-Enfield rifles. During their stay, their officers rotated into the frontline trenches to get firsthand experience. After three weeks of training with the British their orders changed, and they received their American rifles and equipment back. On June 16, the Regiment boarded French 40 × 8 (40 hommes-men, 8 Chevalier-horses) railcars and made a two-day march to the American sector near Toul where they billeted in Lucey.

In this sector, the men of the 328th took their turn in the trenches. On June 26, the 82nd Division relieved the 26th Division, AEF, in a staggered schedule to avoid congestion on the roads and to conceal troop movement. Company G, with the rest of the 2nd Battalion, took over the front that extended from Bouconville to Rambucourt. This area had been relatively quiet in terms of combat, so it allowed the Americans to train in the intricacies of troop movements and relief at night from the trench network. The men also became acquainted with the routine of patrols into "no man's land." This station introduced the men to the difficulty of trench warfare. The work was monotonous, with every day's activities consisting mainly of sitting in a trench staring at the enemy lines without ever seeing a German, getting chow, stringing wire or digging trenches, and conducting nightly patrols. At the end of several weeks, they held the same positions with nothing visibly accomplished.

Their stay in the trenches was not without danger: a few men were killed by nervous sentries and German artillery barrages. Gas held the chief horror for them. Frequently, a zealous gas sentry would sound the gas alarm, filling the whole area with the echoes of horns, bells, and rattles in the middle of the night. Fortunately, to counter the conditions of the front, Regimental Headquarters in Raulecourt had Red Cross, Salvation Army, and YMCA facilities where the men could get hot chocolate and doughnuts on the nights of relief. While this area had relative peace, the men received experience that would give them confidence in the field.

The 89th Division, AEF, relieved the men of the 328th on August 10, 1918. On August 16, the entire 82nd Division moved to relieve the 2nd Division, AEF, in the Marbache Sector. There the men of the 328th moved into Pont-a-Mousson, with the 2nd Battalion again taking the frontline. Fearing a German offensive, the French citizens of the town had fled, leaving luxuriant gardens and orchards with abundant fruit and thereby adding to the company cooks' reputation for resourcefulness in making better meals.

The 82nd remained in this general vicinity until the St. Mihiel Offensive began on September 12, 1918. The men of Company G, 2nd Battalion, received orders to keep in contact with the enemy but remain in their present position, which they did while facing severe resistance. On the morning of September 13, the 2nd Battalion went on the offensive, moving to take the heights north of Norroy. Shortly after dark the men advanced but found no resistance and suffered no casualties.

The 2nd Battalion took the town of Norroy that same day. There they found cooked meals, maps, and military records, all of which indicated that the Germans had left very quickly. After taking their first bit of enemy-held territory, the men passed around German cigars, cigarettes, and beer to celebrate. The next day, on September 14, German aerial observation discovered the 2nd Battalion's position, which resulted in the Germans' heavy shelling of the town and the surrounding territory with high explosives and gas. This intense shelling kept up throughout the afternoon and well into the night, causing the air to be continually filled with gas. The men had to wear their gas masks for more than four hours to avoid a horrible death. The continuous shelling, little rest, and lack of hot food took its toll on the men. Fortunately, the 3rd Battalion relieved the 2nd later that night. The men of Company G moved back to the vicinity of Dieulouard for a much-needed rest.

After the official conclusion of the St. Mihiel Offensive on September 16, 1918, the 82nd returned to service in the Marbache Sector. On September

18, the 328th moved into the Marbache woods south of Belleville. The men
got what little rest they could in the continual rain that lasted throughout
their stay. Due to casualties during the St. Mihiel Offensive, replacements
arrived to fill the ranks in preparation for the Meuse-Argonne Offensive.
On the morning of September 24, the 328th left the Marbache Sector,
with the 2nd Battalion marching to the Argonne Forest and camping at
Camp Mallory on September 26.

Shortly after arriving in the woods, the preliminary barrage com-
menced to signal the start of the Meuse-Argonne Offensive. During
the next few days, the 328th stayed in reserve and while in this position
continued training daily. On October 3, the 328th moved with the 82nd
Division to the vicinity of Losheres where it bivouacked for the night.
They resumed the march the following morning and moved 12 kilome-
ters to take up a position to the east of Camp Mahaut, in the vicinity
of a German cemetery, where they camped. While here they practiced
maneuvers and performed reconnaissance.

Then on the night of October 6, the 328th moved toward Varennes
to join in the fighting. The men marched in the exceptionally dark night
through rain and a mass of traffic on the roads. As the regiment moved
north, the road came under shell fire and a considerable amount of gas.
The 1st Battalion attacked on October 7, with the 2nd Battalion as support. On the morning of October 8, the 2nd Battalion received orders
to continue the advance. The battalion moved out at 02:00 but came
under heavy German artillery fire. The shelling destroyed the only bridge
across the Aire River, forcing the men to ford the badly swollen stream.
They then moved across the intervening valley near Hill 223. Despite
this hardship and numerous casualties from the heavy shelling, the men
got into position before the zero hour and prepared for a battle unaware
that their fight and at least one man would take an important part in the
annals of military history.[5]

On the morning of October 8, sixteen men followed Acting Sgt. Bernard Early on a mission to eliminate German machine gun nests. Later
that day, eleven Americans, four of them wounded, including Early, and
132 German prisoners returned to the American lines. Acting Sgt. Early,
Acting Cpl. Otis Merrithew, Pvt. Mario Muzzi, and Pvt. Patrick Donohue were evacuated in ambulances, and the rest of the patrol marched
their prisoners to Varennes, France. The full story of October 8, 1918, is
discussed in chapter nine as the combination of all the other survivors'
perspectives.

3

The Original Investigation

The day after the battle, October 9, the men who had survived the action unscathed returned to their company, which was now deployed near their objective west of Chatel-Chéhéry—the Decauville Railway. Once they had rejoined the frontlines, the survivors continued fighting in the Argonne Forest. By October 10, 1918, the 328th Infantry Regiment, 82nd Division, stayed on the frontlines despite suffering 718 casualties.[1] Finally, after three weeks of heavy, continuous combat operations during the second and third phases of the Meuse-Argonne Offensive, the 2nd Battalion, 328th Regiment, along with the bulk of the 82nd Division (minus the 157th US Field Artillery Brigade) was finally relieved from the frontlines. Overall, they had suffered 1,189 casualties, or almost 30 percent of the regiment, by the night of October 30, 1918.[2] They were then ordered to move toward the 10th Training Area, US First Army, near the village of Prauthoy, France, for a much-needed period of rest and refit. There they would receive replacements and train for the next phase of the Meuse-Argonne Offensive.

After being relieved, the 328th Regiment moved to a rest area at Camp De Bouzon, near the town of Varennes. It was here that Acting Cpl. Alvin C. York was promoted to the rank of sergeant on November 1, 1918, because of the high number of casualties Company G had sustained during its time in the Argonne.[3] On November 5, Company G, along with the rest of the 2nd Battalion, 328th Regiment, were billeted near the French village of Montigny. After establishing their temporary home, the surviving members of Company G were given either a three- or a seven-day pass to decompress and see the sights of the surrounding area. During these days, replacements began joining the company, and new training schedules were established. However, unbeknownst to members of Company G and the rest of the 328th Regiment, their war was over.[4]

On November 11, 1918, they received word that an armistice had gone into effect at eleven o'clock that morning, suspending armed hostilities. Soon, the men of Company G, 328th Regiment, along with the entire 82nd Division, were on the move again and were eventually billeted outside the French town of Dijon.

While billeted outside Dijon, the story of Sgt. Alvin York's exploits at Chatel-Chéhéry slowly started to emerge. Within the 82nd Division, the story inspired Chaplain (Capt.) John P. Tyler so much that he asked Sgt. York to tell his story to other troops to raise morale. With the permission of his entire chain of command, Sgt. York began a six-week tour telling his version of the October 8 engagement to thousands of American doughboys all over France. Whether he spoke at a YMCA hut or before an entire unit, York had the perfect platform to spread his story.[5] During his tour, Sgt. York was awarded the Distinguished Service Cross (DSC).

It was Capt. Edward C. B. Danforth Jr., commanding officer of Company G, who recommended Sgt. York for the DSC. Danforth's proposal was supported by affidavits from both Pvt. Percy Beardsley and Pvt. Joseph Kornacki. In their affidavits, dated October 23, 1918, Beardsley and Kornacki stated that "Corporal Alvin C. York (1910421), assumed command and with seven other men attacked and captured a machine gun nest taking a number of Machine Guns and 132 prisoners, including four Officers."[6] York received his DSC on November 30, 1918.[7] It should be noted that Kornacki and Beardsley's affidavits in support of York's DSC were not actual eyewitness testimony; rather, they were prepared statements written by their commanding officers.

During the 82nd Division's rest period, Lt. Col. G. Edward Buxton Jr. began research to write the *Official History of 82nd Division American Expeditionary Forces* and sought accounts from the men who had fought on the frontlines.[8] On January 26, 1919, Buxton had Pvts. Percy Beardsley, Patrick Donohue, Michael Sacina, and George Wills sign statements about the October 8 battle. These statements are identical, except for some details surrounding the actual fight. The four men reported that they were taking cover near the captured Germans during the firefight. Thomas Skeyhill later included these statements in his work, *Sergeant York His Own Life and War Diary,* in 1928 and presented them as a part of the later Medal of Honor investigation.[9] These statements, however, do not appear in York's service file. They were also taken ten days before

Capt. Danforth submitted his initial recommendation, so they are not part of any official investigation.[10] During this time, Buxton questioned the surviving men about Early and Merrithew, fully aware that they were in the hospital, but the other patrol members "were not a very articulate lot, and, as is often the case under emergency conditions, had little idea of what happened to anybody except themselves, or what their comrades were doing. Sgt. York alone was able to tell a vivid, continuous story."[11] Thus, York's statement became the basis for the story, which likely became clearer from the many retellings. As Percy Beardsley later remarked, "they asked him [York] what happened and he just sorta gave his version of the story."[12]

On February 5, 1919, Capt. Danforth submitted a request to have Sgt. York's DSC recalled and instead recommended him for the highest award for valor, the Medal of Honor. By 1918, requirements for the Medal of Honor had been revamped in order to ensure that the highest medal for valor did not fall into "undeserving hands." In many cases, too, men had been granted a Distinguished Service Cross but were later found to be entitled to higher recognition.[13] York's case fell into this category, and after going through official battalion, brigade, and divisional channels, it was accepted by Maj. Gen. George B. Duncan, commanding general of the 82nd Division. Duncan then started an investigation into the events involving Sgt. York at Chatel-Chéhéry.[14]

Sandra S. Turner described Maj. Gen. Duncan as York's first press agent. While sitting for his portrait, Duncan told the story of York's single-handed accomplishments to American portrait artist Joseph C. Chase.[15] A few months later, in late January 1919, Duncan told the tale again when the 82nd Division headquarters contacted *Saturday Evening Post* war correspondent, George Pattullo to suggest writing an article about Sgt. York at Chatel-Chéhéry. Pattullo accepted this invitation and traveled to Prauthoy, France, where he joined the official investigating team as they conducted a formal inquiry into Sgt. York's actions.

This investigation became the basis for York's Congressional Medal of Honor and eventual legend about the fight. However, the commanding officers had already made up their minds about York's story. They just needed to ensure that York would receive the Medal of Honor. As Michael Kelly wrote in *Hero on the Western Front: Discovering Alvin York's WWI Battlefield* (2018), "undoubtedly, by this time, the decision had been taken that York should be awarded the Congressional Medal of Honor, and to meet the criteria it was necessary for the higher command to invest in a little embellishment to ensure that the best possible scenario would be presented."[16] This idea is not new. Back in 1927, veterans such as Pvt. Oscar H. Johnson, who served in Company D, 328th Infantry, attributed Sgt. York's publicity to "some higher-up [that] got wind of it and saw an opportunity for some reflected glory."[17] York's chain of command went through the motions of an investigation and had the other survivors sign statements to corroborate their preconceived image of York as a reluctant but conquering hero and one-man army.

This preconceived image is reflected in differences between the affidavits provided for York's DSC and Medal of Honor. As mentioned above, the original DSC statements of October 23, 1918, did not show York working alone. These statements specified that seven other men were still in the fight when York attacked the German position and that they all played roles in the fighting.

The supporting statements of February 6, 1919, for the Medal of Honor were prepared statements that were given to the men to sign, just like the DSC affidavits were. However, they did not mention any other men who were there on October 8th; the statements spoke only of Alvin York.

On the morning of October 8th, 1918, west of Chatel-Chéhéry, Sgt. York performed in action deeds of most distinguished personal bravery and self-sacrifice. His platoon had been sent to the left flank of the assaulting wave, which was then exposed, to clear out some machine guns. Encountering a large machine gun nest all but seven men of his platoon were killed or wounded and all noncommissioned officers, except Sgt. York, who was at that time a Corporal. His comrades had lost hope, but Sgt. York kept his usual balance and self-control. He rallied the men and closed in on the enemy using his rifle as long as he could conveniently reach his ammunition. He then resorted to his pistol with which he killed and wounded no less than fifteen of the enemy. After this intense fight Sgt. York succeeded in taking prisoner the Battalion Commander. Then instructing his seven men he took the remainder of the enemy prisoner in an exceedingly tactful manner. In lining the prisoners up preparatory to taking them to the Battalion P. C. Sgt. York displayed decided decision by placing the officers at the head of the column with himself next in line and the remaining men distributed in the line making it impossible for the enemy to kill any of his men without killing a German.[18]

It is understood that the Congressional Medal of Honor is awarded to a *single* person, not a group, and the official citation for the award does mention "leading seven men."[19] However, these sworn statements from the investigation have been used by some to justify the "single-handed" myth when, in fact, they were not eyewitness statements.

The six affidavits provided by Percy Beardsley, George Wills, Patrick Donohue, Michael Sacina, Feodor Sok, and Joseph Kornacki of February 6 are all identical. [20] As such, they do not represent each individual soldier's perspective. The affidavits must have been prepared and written ahead of time by a commanding officer, and the men were the instructed to sign them. In fact, this is what most of the survivors later asserted. None of the men were personally interviewed for these affidavits, and there was no eyewitness testimony to support the original recommendation for York's Medal of Honor. As Lt. Col. G. Edward Buxton Jr. later pointed out to Otis Merrithew, "decorations are not given out as the result of affidavits made by the person himself, but because of statements made, as a rule, by eyewitnesses of his actions."[21] Yet, this was not the case for Alvin York's Medal of Honor.

Fifteen days later, on February 21, 1919, Pvt. Percy Beardsley and Pvt. George Wills signed another affidavit, which provides a more personal version of the event. This late addition suggests that someone felt the original statements needed more information to sound like personal testimony. This new affidavit is again a prepared statement, which reads close to York's version of events. It gives York the credit for attacking the Germans and taking out a charging enemy column, from front to back. However, Beardsley and Wills were not in the same squad and were physically separate during the battle. Therefore, they would not have seen or experienced the same thing as York during the engagement.[22] The Beardsley and Wills affidavit gives York even more credit for what he did rather than providing any information about the role of the other men.

These statements about York are strange. It is unlikely the men could see, much less later recall, York's actions during the firefight. In fact, several things would have prevented the men from actually knowing what York did. The battle took place in a heavily wooded ravine thick with underbrush. The Americans were scattered and did not have clear sights on any one man outside of their immediate area. During such an intense firefight, the soldiers would have been completely focused on finding cover and either guarding prisoners or fighting back. This is

2nd Bn., 328th Inf.,
32nd Div., American E.F.,
Frettes, France, Feb. 21, 1919.

(Pvt. Percy (1,910,246) Beardsley

AFFIDAVIT OF :

(Pvt. George W. (1,910,418) Wills

      Personally appeared before me the undersigned, Pvt. Percy (1,910,246)
Beardsley and Pvt. George W. (1,910,418) Wills, first being duly sworn according to law, say that they were present with Sergeant Alvin C. (1,910,421) York,
northwest of Chatel-Chehery on the morning of October 8th, 1918, and testified
to the distinguished personal courage, self-sacrifice and presence of mind of
Sgt. Alvin C. (1,910,421) York, as follows:

      "On the morning of the 8th October 1918, Sgt. York was a Corporal in
"G" Company, 328th Infantry and I was a member of his squad. Our Battalion,
the 2nd Battalion of the 328th Infantry was attacking the ridge northwest of
Chatel-Chehery. The battalion had to maneuver across the valley under heavy
machine gun fire which came from our right and left as well as in front of us.
Very heavy fire came from a hill on our left flank. Sgt. Parsons was our platoon leader and he told Acting Sgt. Early to take 3 squads and go over and
clean out the machine guns that were shooting at our left flank. We circled
the hill first in a southerly and then in a southwesterly direction until
the noise of the machine guns sounded as-if the guns were between us and our
battalion. We went down the west slope of the hill into a ravine filled with
heavy underbrush and there found two Germans and fired at one of them when he
refused to halt. We were following the one who ran and came on to a battalion
of Germans grouped together on the bottom of the hill. Those nearest us were
surprised, and thinking they were surrounded started to surrender, but a lot
of machine gunners half way up the hill turned their machine guns on us,
killing six and wounding three of our detachment. All three of our other noncommissioned officers were shot and there was left only Corporal York and seven
privates. We were up against a whole battalion of Germans and it looked pretty
hopeless for us. We were scattered out in the brush, some were guarding a bunch
of Germans who had begun to surrender, and three or four of us fired two or three
shots at the line of Germans on the hillside. The German machine gunners kept
up a heavy fire, as did the German riflemen on the hillside with the machine gunners. The Germans could not hit us without endangering the prisoners whom we
had taken at the very first. A storm of bullets was passing just around and
over us. Corp. York was nearest the enemy and close up to the bottom of the
hill. He fired rapidly with rifle and pistol until he had shot down a German
officer and many of his men. The officer whom Corp. York shot was leading a
charge of some riflemen with bayonets fixed down the hillside towards us.
Finally, the German Battalion Commander surrendered to Corporal York, who called the seven privates remaining up to him and directed us to place ourselves
along the middle and rear of the column of prisoners, which we assisted him in
forming. When we moved out some Germans on a nearby hill continued to fire at
us. Corp. York was at the head of the column where he placed two German officers in front of him. A considerable number of German prisoners were taken
on our way back over the hill. Corp. York made them surrender by having the
German Battalion Commander call to them to give themselves up."

Affidavit of Percy Beardsley and George Wills. Alvin C. York Service Record, NARA.

exactly what York had said to Lt. Col. Edward Buxton. York said he "didn't
know what anybody in the detachment did except himself." [23] Moreover,
Wills, Sacina, and Donohue had been previously interviewed by Buxton
and what they told Buxton is in conflict with the signed affidavits from

the Medal of Honor investigation. As Wills swore: "I only saw Privates Donohue, Sacina, Beardsley, and Muzzi," whereas Sacina testified that "from where I stood, I could not see any of the other men in my detachment because they were hidden from me by the German prisoners." And Donohue swore that "from where I stood, I could only see Privates Wills, Sacina, and Sok."[24] They could not have witnessed York's actions during the firefight, let alone swear to them.

Some of the men who were "interviewed" for these affidavits claimed that they had never given statements and had probably signed any such document by accident. On July 14, 1941, Bernard Early, Otis Merrithew, Percy Beardsley, Patrick Donohue, Joseph Kornacki, and Feodor Sok signed or agreed to have their names used on a letter to the editor of the *Boston Globe* denouncing the movie *Sergeant York*'s portrayal of the events at Chatel-Chéhéry. In the letter, the men said they may have signed the sworn affidavits during the period when they were constantly asked to sign things by their Company Supply Sergeant, such as "a suit of underwear or for a pair of stockings."[25] In addition, not all the men from the patrol were interviewed during the process to award either the DSC or the Medal of Honor. For example, no one questioned Cpl. Early because he had been medically evacuated to the States on January 19, 1919. However, Pvt. Merrithew, Pvt. Muzzi, and Pvt. Johnson were still in France in either their original unit or in hospitals and yet did not have the opportunity to give their stories.

Some of the statements that have signatures are highly suspect. Joseph Kornacki's affidavit for both the DSC and Medal of Honor, and Feodor Sok's affidavit for the Medal of Honor are signed with an "X" as their mark. While some have claimed that the men were illiterate immigrants who could not sign their full names, this is not true. Both Kornacki and Sok had lived in the United States for many years. Both also attended the school that the 82nd Division had established at Camp Gordon to teach English to the many foreign-born recruits with little ability to read or write English.[26]

Sok had been in the United States only three years, yet he could read and write English well enough to sign his draft registration card with his full name on June 5, 1917.[27] Kornacki, on the other hand, faced an interesting dilemma with his signature. He had emigrated to the United States in 1909, and the 1910 census notes that he had enough command of the English language to read and write. Yet his draft registration card is signed with an "X," and his name is written in by another person.[28] It is worth noting that American officers and journalists constantly misspelled his name, and perhaps not even he understood how to properly spell it. Nonetheless, he did attend the English language school at Camp Gordon, and he had full command of his signature by 1919 when the affidavits were produced.

Further, in response to the 1919 affidavit signed with an "X," on October 9, 1929, Kornacki signed the following affidavit regarding his signature.

> I, Joseph Kornacki, of No. 7 Plymouth Place, Holyoke, Mass., on oath depose and say that I was formerly a private first class in Co G, 328th infantry, United States Army, and served with that organization in France during the World War; that while serving in the United States army, I was known as Joseph Konotski, because it was somewhat easier to write that name, and it was apparently easier for the officers and soldiers to pronounce than was my correct name; that my serial number in the United Sates army was No. 1910336; that I was sworn into the army at Camp Devens, Massachusetts, and from the time that I was sworn into service until the time of my discharge, I signed all necessary papers with the name of Joseph Konotski; I was always able to sign my name in writing and never had to sign it by means of any mark; that I was a member of the squad or platoon of soldiers that were present with one Alvin C. York, a member of the above mentioned company, during the Argonne-Meuse battle in France on October 8, 1918, and participated in the battle in which it is claimed through the press and otherwise that said York killed and captured a large number of German soldiers single-handed; that I absolutely deny that I ever signed or executed any affidavit pertaining to that battle, with my mark as a signature, and which affidavit purports to have been executed before on First Lieut. Edwin A. Burkhalter of the above mentioned organization; that to the best of my recollection I never knew any such individual as the said Burkhalter; that during my army service I always signed the payrolls with my signature, as stated above, and not with any mark; that I signed my discharge from the United States army with my signature; that this affidavit is executed voluntarily and in the presence of witnesses and is thoroughly understood.[29]

After entering the service at Camp Gordon and likely because of the school there, Kornacki had learned to sign his own name. In addition, in the case of Kornacki's DSC signature, his name is misspelled both in print and by whoever signed it as "Kornatski."[30]

Supporting the idea that the commanding officers embellished the story to obtain the Medal of Honor for York, the statements were prepared even before the investigators went to the battle site to confirm the story. The original six statements are dated February 6, 1919. The investigation team did not return to the site with York until February 7, 1919. This means that the statements containing York's version of events had already been prepared and signed by the other men before the investigating team had even visited the engagement area to ascertain what had happened. It appears that the chain of command had already made its decision without taking any other evidence or other personal accounts into consideration.

On February 7, 1919, during the journey back to the battle site at Chatel-Chéhéry, Pattullo accompanied the investigating team composed of: Maj. Gen. George B. Duncan, commanding general, 82nd Division, Brig. Gen. Julian R. Lindsey, brigade commander, 164th Brigade, Col. Richard A. Wetherill, regimental commander, 328th Regiment, Maj. James M. Tillman, commanding officer, Regimental Headquarters Co., 328th Regiment, Lt. Col. G. Edward Buxton Jr., Capt. Edward C. B. Danforth Jr., and US Army Signal Corps photographer, Pvt. Frank C. Phillips.[31] No other survivors of the patrol but Sgt. York were invited to participate in the investigation. The officers of the investigating team asked York questions as he retraced his steps and gave his version of what occurred. The same afternoon, Col. Wetherill sent in the recommendation that Alvin York be awarded the Medal of Honor after he had "personally investigated this case."[32] It took only two days from the initial recommendation to the investigation team's confirmation, which is surprisingly short for a so-called thorough investigation.

After the investigation team's confirmation, Capt. Bertrand Cox, commanding officer of Company G, was assigned to determine if the other men who were at Chatel-Chéhéry with York deserved any awards. On October 8, after the patrol's battle in the ravine, Cox had also entered the engagement area while commanding Company F. He came upon the site of the firefight, where they counted between twenty and twenty-five dead Germans.[33] All these fatalities were later attributed to York, notwithstanding the participation of the other sixteen members of the patrol.[34] The War Department would later maintain that "the records do

not show the number of Germans killed by Sergeant York." Nevertheless, the Medal of Honor investigation and subsequent published stories
included the number as fact.[35]

When invited to be part of the official investigation, Cox determined
that the "result of investigation does not justify recommendation for
any of the seven men engaged with Sgt. Alvin C. York." However, when
the report reached Col. Richard Wetherill, commanding officer, 328th
Regiment, he changed the determination to "investigation shows that
men with Sgt. Alvin C. York do not deserve recommendation for DSC
or special mention." Finally, upon reaching Gen. Julian R. Lindsey, commanding general, 164th Brigade, he confirmed that "after personal investigation would not recommend men with Sgt. Alvin C. York for DSC."[36]
This important distinction allowed Lindsey to later recommend some of
the men for awards despite Cox's findings. The Medal of Honor for Sgt.
Alvin York was approved on March 20, 1919.[37]

Why did York's commanders feel the need to embellish his story and
exclude the other men from consideration in the Medal of Honor investigation? One explanation involves York's commanding officers' retention
of their wartime elevated ranks. For the duration of the war, regular US
Army commissioned officers of the rank of colonel or above had been
extraordinarily promoted to higher ranks within the National Army in
order to fulfill the needs of the expanding wartime army. They knew that
when the war was over, they would return to their prewar ranks. This
created an environment in which officers were concerned about securing
both reputations and accolades. Alvin York's commanders were no different. Maj. Gen. George B. Duncan and Brig. Gen. Julian R. Lindsey, both of
whom played major roles in obtaining York's Medal of Honor, continued
to promote York's story after the Armistice and when they returned to the
United States. They would attempt to use York's glory and achievements to
enhance their own reputations as a way to counter the wrath of Maj. Gen.
Hunter Liggett, commanding general, I Corps, which they had incurred
during the second phase of the Meuse-Argonne Offensive.

While in France, Gen. Liggett's aide, Lt. Col. Pierpont L. Stackpole,
kept a personal diary in which he recorded many of the general's meetings and personal thoughts about the officers serving under his command. Between October 6 and October 11, 1918, Liggett repeatedly
expressed growing displeasure with Duncan and Lindsey's leadership of
their respective division and brigade while in the field. On October 7,

Major General George Duncan. Signal Corps Photograph.

Liggett questioned Duncan about his division's poor performance in the crossing of the Aire River. Because of this failure, Stackpole recorded that "Duncan seems to be thick as mud and not worth a damn and neither he nor Sheldon, his chief of staff, seem to have much conception of what they are expected to do in a tactical sense." Liggett then ordered Duncan to capture and hold Hill 223. Duncan gave the task to Lindsey, who proved unable to accomplish this task later that day, to which "General Liggett observed that perhaps some brigade commander would do much better than Lindsey (who seems to have flubbed around all day.)"[38]

This disappointment continued into the fateful day of October 8 with the 2nd Battalion, 328th Regiment's attack on Hill 223. Liggett became "entirely dissatisfied with Duncan and Lindsey . . . and the work of the colonels. Orders have not been carried out properly, handling and maneuvering of troops has been confused and amateurish. He thinks little of Duncan and inclines to the view that Lindsey better go."[39] Thus, the

Brigadier General Julian Lindsey. Signal Corps Photograph.

commanding officers of the 82nd Division fell woefully short of Liggett's expectations on the battlefield.

On October 9, Stackpole recorded that "Duncan's outfit has not moved much if any today and Duncan does not seem to know what he's about anyway—soft, stupid, deceitful." The next day, the reports on the 82nd Division, as recorded by Stackpole, cast Duncan and Lindsey in an even darker light. "The Eighty-second, through Duncan is still more fatigued and about twelve hundred men in all that can be mustered for Lindsey's brigade, the others and many officers being presumably hiding out in the woods or straggling down the quieter paths towards the mess and kitchen. (Duncan thinks he ought to be reinforced, relieved, concerted generally and given a DSC and a city mansion for his distinguished service in bungling everything, standing still and losing his outfit.)" Liggett's concerns about the command climate of both the 164th Brigade and the 82nd Division as a whole had reached such an infuriating point that he thought both officers should be replaced or completely discredited.[40]

On October 11, the commanding general's discontent finally reached a boiling point after an altercation between Col. Frank D. Ely, regimental commander, 327th Regiment, and Brig. Gen. Julian Lindsey. Lindsey had replaced Col. Ely with the 327th's regimental executive officer, Lt. Col. Frank H. Burr, after the battle of Cornay, France. Col. Ely then reported directly to Gen. Liggett at his headquarters and claimed that they had long-standing animosity toward each other. As historian Robert Ferrell said, "the tempest between Colonel Ely and Brigadier General Julian R. Lindsey showed how uncertain were commanders in their reputations with their seniors, this at a time when the Meuse-Argonne's second attack had failed. Lindsey was in trouble with Liggett."[41]

Fortunately, on October 12, Gen. Liggett was promoted to Lt. Gen. and was given command of the US First Army.[42] Although Gen. Liggett had been promoted out of the division, the damage to the reputations of Duncan, Lindsey, and the regimental commanders serving under them had already been done.

However, Alvin York and his story might be just the thing to burnish their tarnished images. Promoting his Medal of Honor recommendation

Major General Hunter Liggett. Library of Congress Prints and Photographs Division.

might help them show that they had not bungled the operation. Instead of being the biggest failure of command in Liggett's eyes, Hill 223 could be chalked up as a success. Perhaps their support for Alvin York's story contributed to Duncan and Lindsey later receiving the Distinguished Service Medals for their leadership of the 82nd Division.[43]

On April 11, 1919, Sgt. York was formally awarded the Congressional Medal of Honor.[44] He would also be awarded the French Legion of Honor, French Military Medal, French 1914–1918 Croix de Guerre with Palm, Italian War Merit Cross, and Order of Prince Danilo I from Montenegro. His official citation states that he received the Medal of Honor for

> conspicuous gallantry and intrepidity above and beyond the call of duty in action with the enemy near Chatel Chéhéry, France, October 8, 1918. After his platoon had suffered heavy casualties and three other noncommissioned officers had become casualties, Corporal York assumed command. Fearlessly leading seven men, he charged with great daring a machinegun nest which was pouring deadly and incessant fire upon his platoon. In this heroic feat the machinegun nest was taken, together with four officers and 128 men and several guns.[45]

Further promoting York's actions were two articles about him that hit the newsstands in April 1919. The April issue of *World's Work* included the brief statement about York at the end of an article written by Joseph Cummings Chase.[46] This article did not get as much attention as George Pattullo's article, "The Second Elder Gives Battle," which appeared in the *Saturday Evening Post* on April 26, 1919.[47] At the time, the *Saturday Evening Post* had a circulation of two million, making it the most widely read magazine in the United States.[48] Pattullo's article pushed Sgt. York's story into the spotlight. Unfortunately, however, it is based exclusively on York's version of the events and did not consider the perspective of the other men. Pattullo later claimed that he had talked to "every surviving member of the platoon,"[49] a claim that some of the men, such as Otis Merrithew refuted: "I never heard of Pattullo. He never spoke to me."[50]

Pattullo's article reflected what George Seldes had said about press correspondents searching for romanticized images for the wartime press. More recently, Sandra Turner says that "through the mingling of facts, a bit of romanticizing, and much personal opinion, Pattullo creates for Americans an image of the outstanding hero of the war."[51] He, in a sense, created the York legend by making York famous. Pattullo glorified York and his exploits to fit a mold of an idealized American hero. Pattullo emphasized York's humble origins as a miscreant who found religion. He also described how York was transformed from a conscientious objector into a God-fearing Christian warrior, and he presented York's perspective of how the battle of Chatel-Chéhéry unfolded. Pattullo's description of York's actions captured the American imagination and in a larger sense supported the United States' involvement in the war. Like York, the country had been reluctant to get into the hostilities but was determined to finish. Military and civilian leaders welcomed this rationalization, since the US entry into a European war was by no means universally popular. As the *Sunday Republican* noted in 1927, "George Pattullo . . . had as much to do with creating York's reputation as anyone."[52]

Unfortunately, like the investigation, Pattullo's article also showed the hand of York's commanding officers in shaping the narrative of the battle. Maj. Gen, Duncan had control over what Pattullo could publish. In a speech at the Tennessee Society's banquet for York on May 23, 1919, Duncan told the crowd that "as to the facts of Sergt. York's exploit, they are already in your possession, as you have all read of them adequately in the public press and more specifically in the article by George Pattullo in the Saturday Evening Post." Duncan then told the group how he warned Pattullo to get every detail accurate as "they must go down in history."[53] Alvin York confirmed that Duncan had the final say on Pattullo's article. York told a crowd in Knoxville, Tennessee, that Pattullo's article "is an accurate account of the story. It was taken from the military officers. The commanding officer would not let it be published unless it was taken from the military records, and affidavits or officers who were acquainted with the facts."[54] Since the officers had decided to expand and exaggerate York's version of the battle, that is the story Pattullo wrote. This control and mishandling of the actual story are shown in the censor's copy of Pattullo's article. Originally, Pattullo had written that York killed twenty-five Germans but changed it to twenty for the final printing. Likewise, Pattullo claims that the investigation lasted a week, yet in reality it only took two days.[55] Ultimately, his article thrust York's actions into the spotlight and brought national fame to the mountain man. None of this would spread to the other sixteen men, for an acknowledgment of assistance would undermine York's heroism.

Perhaps the most concerning aspect of this incident is that even though a few of the other men had received some recognition for their roles in the battle, they would be left out as the legend grew in the popular media back in the United States. As noted earlier, Sgt. York's Medal of Honor citation mentioned the participation of seven other soldiers.[56] The official Signal Corps photograph of York taken on February 7, 1918, included the description "with the aid of 17 men."[57] But these references would become fewer as the legend grew from the investigation and subsequent press coverage.

Five of the men were officially cited for gallantry in action, which awarded them a Silver Citation Star Certificate that entitled them to place a small 3/16th Silver Star device on their World War I Victory Medal and, after 1932, allowed them to obtain the Silver Star Medal. Four privates, Percy Beardsley, Joseph Kornacki, George Wills, and Patrick Donohue, were officially cited for gallantry in action in General Orders No. 1, Headquarters, 164th Brigade, 82nd Division, dated Sunday, May 4, 1919. Pvt. Michael Sacina was also commended for gallantry in action at Chat-el-Chéhéry on October 8, 1918, in General Orders No. 11, Headquarters, 328th Regiment, 164th Brigade, 82nd Division.[58]

Percy Beardsley's citation read: "During the attack on Hill 180, west of Chatel-Chéhéry, Mechanic Beardsley with a detachment from his company surprised and captured a number of Germans, who were delivering flanking fire on the attacking line." Pvt. Kornacki, Pvt. Wills, and Pvt. Donohue all received an identical citation: "On October 8, 1918, in action west of Chatel-Chéhéry this soldier when his company was held up by the enemy flanking fire, with several others crawled to the flank and killed or captured the enemy who were delivering the flanking fire."[59]

Despite this official acknowledgment of the roles other survivors played, the story grew into a legend in which Alvin York "single-hand-edly" captured 132 Germans and silenced 32 machine guns. This descrip-tion did not sit well with several members of the patrol and other soldiers of the regiment who began to contest this version of events as early as their return to the United States in 1919.[60] It would have been extremely difficult for Sgt. Alvin York to extricate himself from this claim, as Maj. Gen. Duncan accompanied him to speaking events held in his honor. York kept to his story and stated that their affidavits gave him the credit for the awards.[61]

Other veterans also contested York's claims when they returned home. On June 15, 1919, a soldier from Chattanooga, Tennessee, expressed concern about calling York the "greatest" hero of the war. "I know all about Sergt. York's wonderful performance and his heroic deed, as I was in the same sector in France when it took place. But I also know of numerous other heroic acts . . . it is an injustice to the numerous other heroes who have gone through three times the service and did as much when all summed up as Sergt. York."[62] Some men who had been proud that York served in their unit became disillusioned when they heard about his heroics. In a book that he wrote after the war, 2nd. Lt. Frank A. Holden, who served in the 328th Infantry Regiment, 82nd Division, said: "I would not go two blocks to hear Sergeant Alvin York tell of how he killed twenty Germans and captured one hundred and thirty-two, and I doubt if there are many others who would."[63] Although the reactions of other veterans attracted some press coverage, they remained footnotes to the accepted myth that continued to thrive.

The myth of Sgt. Alvin York had been created because commanding officers, especially Maj. Gen. Duncan, promoted and inflated it for their own advantage. The investigation team and George Pattullo laid the foundation for a tale of "single-handed" action that would captivate the American people. However, the other survivors could not accept that their shared experience could be pushed aside. They began to find ways to speak out against the myth.

4

The War College

After returning home to Pall Mall, Tennessee, Sgt. York continued to spread his story across the country during tours to raise money for a planned bible school in Tennessee. When York spoke in Boston on January 28, 1920, Otis Merrithew attended the event. This may have surprised York, who like the other members of the patrol probably believed Cutting [Merrithew] had died of his wounds. York brought Merrithew on stage and introduced him as "Boston's hero" and told the crowd that Merrithew served with him at the battle of the Argonne.[1] This was the first and only time that York would willingly bring another member of the patrol before the public.

Despite the lack of public recognition from York, Lt. Col. G. Edward Buxton Jr., battalion commander, 328th Regiment, 82nd Division, and author of the official 82nd Division history helped Bernard Early gain recognition. Buxton began the effort to have Early recognized for his leadership and role in the October 8, 1918, engagement after hearing his story.[2] While speaking about the American Legion in Norwich, Connecticut, on February 20, 1920, Buxton said the people of Connecticut should feel endless pride that

> the man who commanded that little expedition of seventeen; who led them by an exceedingly skillful reconnaissance around the enemy flank, who made the decision to attack irrespective of what the enemy numbers might be, and who was shot down by a machine gun in the fight that followed with three bullets in his back and one through his arm—that man was a citizen of your state, and I rejoice that Sergeant Bernard Early is nearly recovered from his terrible wounds and

is now living in your city of New Haven. Furthermore, it is my hope that I may succeed in securing for Early that full recognition from the military authorities which is his due and which will in no measure detract from the great honor justly accorded to his comrade York.[3]

Buxton's effort did get the American Legion involved in a push to award Early the DSC for his actions. The Legion's support of Early also reportedly led York to cancel speaking engagements in New Haven because Early was also invited and might have challenged York's claims.[4] This led some to interpret York's cancellation as an indication that York feared having the truth about the engagement revealed, namely, that it was not a one-man show.[5]

Lt. Col. Buxton also took his support for Early to the War Department, writing a recommendation to George B. Duncan, the former 82nd Division commander, who then transmitted it to the War Department.[6] Buxton believed that Early had been "robbed of the fruits of his victory by the surprise fire from the hillside overhead" and hoped to finally see him justly awarded.[7] Duncan then addressed his letter directly to Gen. Robert C. Davis, adjutant general, who replied that to be awarded, Early would need two eyewitness accounts. Buxton relayed this information to Early and requested the names of those who could support his claims.[8] However, the resulting recommendation was soon filed away and ignored because they could not get an affidavit from Alvin York to support it. [9] The failure of both the government agencies and York to act or provide an affidavit became a routine problem for the other men attempting to secure recognition in the 1920s.

Throughout the 1920s, stories about the role of the other sixteen men appeared in local newspapers but did not receive much attention beyond their home states. Meanwhile, York's fame grew. His honors included the gift of a 400-acre farm by the Rotary Club of Nashville, Tennessee.[10] During the latter half of the decade, Otis Merrithew applied to have his named changed from William Cutting in the War Department records. He wanted to join the local American Legion post but could not because of the name difference in his official paperwork.[11] He did not publicize or call attention to his service at this time.

It was not until May 1927, when the *American Legion Monthly* magazine ran an article about the other members of the patrol, that the men received their first bit of national recognition. The article was written after Pvt. Oscar H. Johnson of Galesburg, North Dakota, who served in Company D, 328th Infantry, wrote to criticize the magazine for failing to mention the other men in an article about York in their February 1927 issue. Johnson said that "credit should be given where credit is due."[12] In response to Johnson, the American Legion looked into the 82nd Division's history and found that "the records show that six men are mentioned in connection with the conduct of Sgt. Alvin C. York."[13] The article then listed the names of the other men and their citations.

Recognition in the *American Legion Monthly* kicked off a search to find these other men who had been almost completely forgotten. The *Sunday Republican* of Roxbury, Connecticut, tracked down Percy Beardsley who lived in the town. On May 27, 1927, the newspaper published an article about his role in the engagement. The *Republican* also reported that Sgt. York had canceled a lecture in Waterbury, Connecticut, after hearing that Beardsley had also been invited to the lecture.[14] Beardsley often argued that Bernard Early should have received a medal for the action because he had been in charge that morning.[15] Increasingly, the other men felt that Alvin York intentionally avoided them, which made it impossible for them to receive the honor they deserved.

In the fall of 1929, the US Army War College located at Washington Barracks in Washington, DC, created an opportunity for all the men to come together and, although it was certainly not the Army's intention, tell their version of events. From Thursday, October 3, to Saturday, October 5, 1929, the Annual Military Exposition and Carnival was to be held at the Army War College. The event would re-create select events of the Meuse-Argonne Offensive in a mock battle, which would show what had occurred at Chatel-Chéhéry with Sgt. Alvin C. York. The finale of the three-day event was to be a dramatic event called "Smashing Through the Argonne with Sergeant York" in which the War College would act out how York performed his daring feat.[16]

The creator of the reenactment, Capt. Henry Swindler, would have to research the participant's accounts in order to reconstruct the battle. He discovered that these accounts were far from consistent. As historian David D. Lee points out, "unfortunately, their [the participants] memories reflected the chaos of the moment, making it almost impossible to reconstruct the situation exactly. Although the Army collected affidavits from several participants just a few months after the incident." [17] Swindler discovered that "the statements of various people concerned are quite conflicting."[18] He also sought the truth in *Sergeant York: His Own Life Story and War Diary*, edited by Tom Skeyhill and published in 1928. However, Swindler continued to find problems with the story. In trying to figure out what actually happened with the German bayonet charge, Capt. Edward C. B. Danforth Jr. told Swindler that he and Maj. Buxton agreed that "the bayonet attack . . . was not a concerted action by the whole of the enemy force but merely a rush by some five or six Germans that had succeeded in getting to within thirty or forty yards of York."[19] Inconsistencies in the story proved to be a challenge in faithfully reenacting the battle.

The program for the event contained several pages dedicated to retelling the York story and how he performed his feat alone. Some historians have argued that York and the Army did not create the "single-handed" myth. Rather, it was created by an overly enthusiastic media whose primary intention was to sell magazines and newspapers. For example, Col. Douglas V. Mastriano, USA Ret., author of *Alvin York: A New Biography of the Hero of the Argonne*, claims that "neither York nor the U.S. Army made such bold assertions."[20] However, the US Army War College's official program for the "exposition and carnival" included an article written by Maj. Robert. B. Lawrence who began the story by asking, "How did he do it? How could one man, with practically no assistance, kill 25 men, silence a battalion of the enemy's guns, capture 4 officers and 128 prisoners, and lead them back through an enemy-infested forest to his own lines?"[21] The US Army was now officially acknowledging and perpetuating the York legend. In addition, autographed copies of *Sergeant York: His Own Life Story and War Diary* were sold during the event to earn money for the Alvin C. York Agricultural Institute in Jamestown, Tennessee.[22]

To advertise this carnival, the US Army invited the other survivors to attend. Most of the ten survivors who received invitations had not seen each other since returning to the United States after the war. Michael Sacina and Thomas Johnson were invited but could not be reached. Feodor Sok received his invitation but not the money the Army was supposed to provide for transportation. Not being able to afford to come, he missed the event.[23] Percy Beardsley originally declined the invitation because it conflicted with the sale of cattle from his farm, and he needed to be present. However, he seems to have found a way to attend.[24] Bernard Early, Joseph Kornacki, George W. Wills, and Patrick J. Donohue did accept the invitation to attend. However, Donohue was ultimately unable to do so because of his job. Otis B. Merrithew also received an invitation since he had changed the official record of his name. This was a surprise for his former squad mates who thought he had died of his wounds since they could not find "William Cutting" after the war. Maj. Gen. George B. Duncan, and Maj. Edward C. B. Danforth Jr. also attended the event.[25]

The invitations sent out on Monday, September 16, 1929, read, in part:

> This year we will show the action of the 82nd Division in the Argonne and as a part of the sham battle, we will show the destruction of the machine gun nests and the capture of prisoners when Sergeant Alvin C. York so distinguished himself. Sergeant York is coming to the show and will be here for the three days. *We would like to have you, as one of the survivors of this fight, come also.*
>
> We will pay all expenses of this trip, show you an exceedingly good time and you will have a chance to meet some of your old buddies.[26]

As the newspapers began to report on the event, the men's stories got more recognition. Early, who had previously spoken out against York's one-man army, got the most attention. Both Merrithew and Beardsley supported and agreed with Early's rendition of the events of October 8, 1918.[27]

A *Boston Globe* reporter interviewed Bernard Early on September 30, 1929, before he left for Washington, DC. In the interview, Early discussed his version of the story and reiterated that Sgt. Alvin York never appeared in public when invited to speak at events if other survivors were present. "I've never seen him since that morning over there on the edge of the Argonne Forest and I don't think I'll see him this year either." Early also showed his frustration with York, saying: "I don't blame him for grabbing all the glory he can, but the thing that riles me up is the fact that he got credit for something that seven other men had as much of a part in. I'm not looking for anything for myself, but I would like to see that the other fellows got proper recognition." The article then reported that both Early and Beardsley would try to get the other men some recognition at the War College's event.[28]

Another *Boston Globe* reporter then interviewed Merrithew about the statements that both Early and Beardsley had made. Merrithew said that Early's version of the story was "correct in every detail." He then added that he was sorry that Early was anxious to get recognition for the other men but not for himself. Merrithew said: "Early was a great soldier. . . . It was Early's command that brought us across the open spaces safely, and for that he deserves all the credit in the world."[29] Because of this comment, the Army War College saw Merrithew as a problem for the event. In an interview in the *Boston Herald*, Merrithew said: "I am not looking for the glory. But York has been drummed up and down the country as a one-man army. What about the other men in the unit? Early in particular for the way he used his head in getting us into the woods without a casualty. Early surely deserves a medal and I think all the men deserve the same for the buck privates fired just as many shots as York."[30]

Inclement weather postponed Merrithew, Early, and Beardsley's arrival at the carnival by plane, but their stories spread across the country.[31] The contradictions and public attention brought new controversy and claims from other veterans. York first responded to Early and Beardsley on October 2. Incredibly, York claimed "I am not acquainted with either Early or Beardsley and I can't imagine what their purpose is in attacking my record. My exploits during the war are all on file with the War Department. I can't understand what they have against me."[32] Next, officials at the War Department weighed in, claiming that it would need proof that Merrithew, Early, and Beardsley deserved special recognition. War Department officials indicated that the official records gave Sgt. York the credit and that it would be necessary to show strong evidence to cause any change. Surprised War Department officials, who were clearly caught flat-footed by the response of the other men, also specifically stated that there was no record that either Bernard Early or Otis Merrithew had taken any part in the exploit.[33] Rather than offer to review the claims of the other men, the officials at the Army War College were angry at Early, Merrithew, and Beardsley: "They are coming here as our guests. Surely common courtesy would rule out any such disturbance at this time." The officials intimated that, had they known of this dissension a few days earlier, they might even have withdrawn their invitations.[34] The York legend clearly trumped the truth for the US Army.

Former Plt. Sgt. Harry Parsons also spoke negatively to reporters about Early's claims, even though he was not in the ravine on October 8, 1918. Parsons said that "credit belongs entirely to York" and even insinuated that Early was "careless and may have been shot down because he made it a practice to stand up foolishly while not under cover."[35] To further his point, Parsons asked reporters: "If a man finds gold but is attacked by robbers and someone else beats off the robbers and brings in the gold, who deserves credit? That is the situation regarding that exploit in the Argonne."[36] To that, survivors might argue that the man who found the gold should get credit for finding it, and the man who beat off the robbers should get credit for that. There is enough credit to share, rather than one man taking it all. Of course, it should be remembered that Parsons selected Early to lead the patrol, which could be described as a suicide mission. It was hardly a job for a foolish soldier.

Other veterans began to voice their opinions. Former Pfc. Saul Odess of Fall River, Massachusetts, claimed he was a part of the platoon and wanted to be invited to the War College event. He even had a congressman take up the matter.[37] However, the War Department found absolutely no evidence showing that Odess was part of the platoon in the engagement.[38] Former Cpl. Sarkis Parigian, who served as a squad leader with Company E, 2nd Battalion, 328th Regiment, claimed that his company was also present that day and had surrounded the entire hill when the Germans were laying down their weapons. Parigian argued that "if there are honors and medals to be given out, then members of the companies which fought early in the engagement, also should get their share of glory." Former Cpl. Parigian himself was cited twice in two General Orders for capturing an enemy machine gun position that held seven enemy machine guns, and for aiding in the capture of a fortified enemy position that held seven German and forty American soldiers who had been taken prisoner just days before. Parigian never received any official awards for his acts of valor, though he would qualify for the Silver Star Medal instituted three years later in 1932.[39]

On the morning of Thursday, October 3, 1929, Bernard Early and Percy Beardsley arrived in Washington, DC, joining Joseph Kornacki and George W. Wills who had arrived days earlier. At the War College, Early and Beardsley were met by Col. Leon B. Kromer who urged them to refrain from any further discussion of the controversy until after the close of the carnival. Kromer's intervention came after high-ranking War Department officials had a private conference with both former Plt. Sgt. Harry Parsons and Gen. Charles P. Summerall, chief of staff, US Army. After this meeting, Parsons revealed that they would be awarding decorations at the event and "everything will be lovely and everyone satisfied." Parsons also said that former Sgt. Alvin C. York may not be "wholly satisfied with an official action which will take from him the credit he has so long enjoyed of effecting a 'one-man capture' of more than 100 of the enemy." Fortunately, "York is a great soldier and . . . he will acquiesce without protest in whatever action is taken in the official recognition of his former comrades."[40] Reporter Thomas Carens wrote about the War Department's attempts to downplay the other survivors, saying: "In spite of frantic attempts of the department, and particularly of officers in charge of the military carnival at the War College, to hush the whole affair up, it was reported tonight that on Saturday afternoon decorations will be awarded to all eight survivors of the engagement at a ceremony in which York himself will be a participant."[41]

Otis B. Merrithew arrived in Washington, DC, that night to join the other men at the event. When he arrived, Col. Kromer also urged him not to speak out during the event. The "diplomat hinted at the coming decorations and urged Merrithew to keep quiet if he did not feel like radiating joy and peace."[42] However, as Merrithew said to his wife in a letter "I could have started a real war down here, but this show is for a good cause and I don't think anybody back home would like me to do that."[43]

Otis Merrithew leaving for US the Army War College. Courtesy of Jimmy Fallon.

The announcement of decorations quieted the men for the day. The insurgency that threatened to ruin the carefully planned and advertised program appeared to be under control. According to reporters, all seemed happiness and harmony down at the War College. Parsons did tell the press that Early and Beardsley were staying at a local hotel, rather than the quarters provided for them at the War College because they "preferred such an arrangement." Parsons then denied that they had been asked to stay at the hotel because of their criticisms of the event.[44]

Thomas Carens reported more details on the tense evening, saying that "while Konotsky is dining with York and a select group at the War College, Merrithew, Early, and Beardsley, whose recent newspaper statements have caused so much resentment, are in other parts of the city." He also revealed that "although Early and Beardsley were scheduled to remain at the War College, they departed later in the day for the business section of Washington and registered at a hotel. No explanation was given for their unwillingness to remain at the War College with their comrades, and it was assumed they found the resentment there a little too keen."[45] Otis Merrithew agreed with the other men and stayed at the Mayflower Hotel in Washington instead of the War College.[46]

On Friday, October 4, 1929, the War Department formally announced that its regulations would be an obstacle in giving all the men their due recognition. The department said it would only award one of the survivors a decoration, although the others might or might not receive a citation in the future. The time for awarding the Medal of Honor, Distinguished Service Cross, and Distinguished Service Medal had expired on May 26, 1928.[47] Any future decoration requests sent to the War Department after that date would need special congressional permission, unless the intended recipient had been recommended prior to the expiration date. This law would prove an insurmountable barrier to awarding decorations to Otis Merrithew and other patrol members in the years to come. Some of the men were clearly unhappy with this announcement. Merrithew showed his displeasure by not attending the War College on October 4.[48] To dampen the discontent, War Department officials took great pains to keep the members of the Chatel-Chéhéry patrol away from each other and from Sgt. York. Department officials also planned to announce their decision at the end of the event to avoid interfering with the exposition.[49]

On Saturday, October 5, 1929, the War Department formally announced that it would award former Cpl. Bernard Early the DSC for his actions on October 8, 1918. The US Army's Awards and Decoration Board had held a special session the day before and recommended that Secretary of War James W. Good approve the awarding of the DSC and that it be presented to Sgt. Early in person at the closing of the War College exposition. The War Department used the recommendation letter from Lt. Col. G. Edward Buxton Jr that had been in its files since 1920 as the basis for its decision to award the medal to Early. This letter, which had been filed away and ignored, called attention to the "belief held by many officers and men of the brigade to which the 328th Infantry was attached, that Early as the noncommissioned officer who gave the original order to advance with seventeen men against the German stronghold held by 200 Germans, should have been given the DSC. Some held that he should have received the Congressional Medal of Honor along with York without detracting from York's feat."[50]

The original recommendation letter was addressed to Gen. Robert C. Davis, who recommended that efforts be made to get sworn affidavits from both Sgt. York and the surviving members of the patrol who took part in the engagement. These sworn affidavits never materialized, "presumably because of a dispute between Sgt. Early and Sgt. York," which meant Sgt. Early did not receive a decoration.[51] Fortunately, Secretary of War James W. Good, said that Bernard Early's actions had been overlooked in the heat of battle and that they well deserved recognition.[52] Capt. Edward C. B. Danforth added a recommendation to Buxton's to establish the claim for Early's award. It read:

> The advance of his company being held up in the valley west of Hill 223 in the vicinity of Chatel-Chéhéry, France, by converging enemy machine gunfire from the front and both flanks, Corporal Early led a detachment of 17 men, sent from a support platoon, with the mission of silencing the hostile fire on our left flank. He skillfully moved his men through the sparsely wooded country to a position on the left of and somewhat beyond our lines, coming suddenly upon a group of some 50 to 75 of the enemy in a small clearing. Though greatly outnumbered, in a dangerous situation, in which he risked annihilation, he courageously opened fire with his small detachment and forced the surrender of the enemy group. While giving instructions for taking the prisoners to the rear, he was shot down with three bullets through the body in a storm of fire of enemy machine guns, from the hill to his rear, which killed six and wounded two other of his men.

He later walked out, aided by the survivors of his detachment, now under command of Corporal Alvin C. York, who had silenced and captured the remaining enemy guns and gunners, while he (Early) was out of action.[53]

With these two recommendations and the support of the secretary of war, Early could finally receive his award.

On the afternoon of October 5, 1929, Bernard Early was finally presented the DSC for his leadership and handling of the seventeen-man patrol while at Chatel-Chéhéry, France, on the morning of Tuesday, October 8, 1918. Early was awarded in front of thousands of cheering civilians, soldiers, congressmen, and military officials. When it was announced that he was receiving the DSC, Early was escorted onto the field by soldiers from the 3rd US Cavalry Regiment, who came to a halt and stood at attention opposite the reviewing stand. The national anthem of the United States played as Early and the throng of attendees arose and stood silently. Early held a stiff and precise salute until the last notes faded away. Assistant Secretary of War Patrick J. Hurley and his aide approached Early. The aide read the citation aloud while Secretary Hurley pinned the DSC onto Early's proud chest.[54] His citation read:

> The President of the United States of America, authorized by Act of Congress, July 9, 1918, takes pleasure in presenting the Distinguished Service Cross to Formerly Corporal (Acting Sergeant) Bernard Early, Co. G, 328 Infantry, 82nd Division, American Expeditionary Forces, for extraordinary heroism in action near Chatel-Chéhéry, France, October 8, 1918. When in command of a party of 17 men Sergeant Early flanked a German battalion. Upon being suddenly confronted by about 200 of the enemy Sergeant Early decided to attack despite the disparity of numbers. By his quick decision and excellent leadership Sergeant Early effected a successful surprise attack, which he led and commanded until severely wounded by enemy machine-gun fire. The conspicuous gallantry and outstanding leadership on the part of Sergeant Early so inspired the remainder of his small command that it continued the attack until the enemy battalion was either killed or taken prisoner.[55]

With the completion of this ceremony, Early was escorted back to the reviewing stand to sit beside Assistant Secretary of War Hurley. Senator

Asst. Sec. War Patrick J. Hurley congratulating Sgt. Bernard Early after decorating him with
D.S.C. Army Relief Carnival, Oct. 5, 1929. Signal Corps Photograph.

Frederic Walcott of Connecticut hurried over to congratulate Early and
perhaps best expressed the feelings about this belated award. "I take my
hat off to you," he told Early. "Anyone who deserves one of those, and
you certainly deserve one, should be congratulated with bared head."[56]

After the event, Early returned to his home in New Haven where he
attended various celebrations. He accompanied an outing of soldiers from
Company B, 1st Battalion, 102nd Infantry Regiment, 85th Brigade, 43rd
Infantry Division, Connecticut National Guard, and received a rousing
ovation from war veterans and others who attended the event.[57] The city
of New Haven planned "Sergeant Early Day" for Saturday, October 12,
1929.[58] Despite the fame and attention, Early remained modest, saying
"I'm not much on this hero stuff. Down at Washington I went through
something that was worse than that scrap on Hill 223 when they stood
me up in front of 10,000 people, all alone to pin that cross on me. And I
have a feeling that I'm going to feel the same way today."[59]

Bernard Early Day began with a massive parade in honor of Early.
Many military units, bands, veterans from both the Spanish-American

War and World War I, Veterans of Foreign Wars posts, and various city groups lined up to march through the city. Early and Otis Merrithew reviewed the parade with an escort of other DSC recipients.[60] The day

AUGUST EIRICH, Jr., Gen. Chairman   HERBERT L. EMANUELSON, Sec'y   EDWARD L. O'NEIL, Treas.

Bernard Early Day

SATURDAY, OCTOBER 12, 1929

205 Church Street
New Haven, Connecticut
October 8, 1929

Mr. Otis Merrithew
267 Boylston Street
Brookline, Mass.

My dear Mr. Merrithew:

    The citizens of New Haven are planning to do honor to Sergeant Bernard Early, a native and lifelong resident of this city, on Saturday, October 12, 1929. Last week, in the nation's capitol, Sergeant Early received from the government the Distinguished Service Cross for his noteworthy service in the cause of liberty in the World War. To-day Sergeant Early lives in our midst, a modest hero, severely wounded, and his many friends feel that the least they can do is to appropriately honor him on the occasion of his receiving this distinction, which he has so long deserved.

    Saturday, October 12th, has therefore been designated as "Bernard Early Day" and will be celebrated by a parade in the afternoon at 3:30, in which many civic organizations will be represented and all the New Haven military organizations. At 6:00 o'clock a banquet will be given in his honor at the Hotel Garde and it is the sincere hope of the committee that you will find it possible to be present at both of these functions. We earnestly urge you to make a special effort to be present at the banquet.

    I am herewith enclosing one ticket for the banquet, which is sent to you with the compliments of the committee. Will you kindly advise me by return mail whether you will be able to be present at both of these affairs. The parade starts at the Armory at 3:00 o'clock, and if you will let me know the train on which you will arrive, I will be glad to have a representative meet you.

Very sincerely yours,

Herbert L. Emanuelson

Secretary of the Committee.

Invitation to celebrate Bernard Early Day in New Haven, Connecticut. Courtesy of Jimmy Fallon.

ended with a testimonial dinner. York, Merrithew, Lt. Col. Buxton, and Beardsley were all invited to attend the banquet. However, only Merrithew and Beardsley attended. Lt. Col. Buxton sent a telegram expressing his regret for not being able to attend.[61]

This banquet drew so much attention and demand for tickets that the venue was changed to the Hotel Garde in order to hold the hundreds of attendees.[62] At the banquet, Thomas A. Tully, mayor of New Haven, presented Early with the City Service Medal. Connecticut Lieutenant Governor Earnest E. Rogers presented Early with the State of Connecticut Service Medal and $400 that had been raised by subscription.[63] In showing his appreciation to those present, Early's modest speech simply said: "My words cannot express the feeling I have in my heart."[64] Early had finally received the hero's welcome and recognition that had been denied him eleven years before.

The presentation of the DSC to Early was a climax to the hectic week, which the War Department had tried so diligently to keep calm. Even though Early had finally received the long overdue credit he so rightly deserved, the other surviving members of the patrol did not get similar attention, especially Otis B. Merrithew. Likewise, the other survivors patiently awaited action on their claims after being told that War Department officials would make sure "everyone will be taken care of."[65] But events unfolded in such a way that Alvin York was still given the largest share of credit for the events that occurred at Chatel-Chéhéry in October 1918. Early's citation gave him credit for inspiring York to perform his feat. However, the other men were never given any sort of official citation for their own heroic part. As the *Hartford Courant* noted, "the War Department continues to play the game of secrecy and mystery . . . now intimates that it will be well-nigh impossible to give awards to the others."[66]

The War College event showed the War Department "displaying politics and an effort to quiet the insurgency that threatened to ruin its military exposition."[67] Reporters also commented on the peculiar circumstances that had led the War Department to finally admit that Bernard Early had already been recommended for an award for his heroic part in the actions at Chatel-Chéhéry by his superiors and other soldiers ten years prior, in 1920. Only after the men's stories became national news did the War Department recognize the validity of the request for recognition.

Reporter Bulkley S. Griffin, the man who originally told the Army officers about Early's comments on York, wrote an article after the event that called attention to the War Department's actions. He noted:

> The War Department played a common garden variety of politics this week. That is a flat statement and a strong statement but it seems the only fit characterization of the department's performance in dealing with the efforts of the members of Sergeant York's outfit in the Argonne to secure credit for others of the survivors besides York. Anything that is written here intends in no way to detract from the glory and honor due Sergeant Bernard Early of New Haven. He was recommended for a medal about 10 years ago, but he never got it till today, and it can be believed that he never would have got it today had not the War Department been much alarmed by reports that Early and others threatened to disrupt the harmony of the military exposition this week by carrying down here their efforts for recognition.
>
> By giving Early a medal—which no one is saying he does not deserve—and by hinting that the others of the outfit would get medals or citations, the department managed to quell the storm and secure a serene front for its annual advertisement of the Army—for that is what the military exhibition constitutes and is intended to constitute.
>
> Whether certain Army officers, in informal intimations, played a sharp trick on the seven others who so far have got nothing but hints, is a moot question. Naturally none of them cares to reply in the affirmative so long as they think they have [a] chance of getting an award, but the fact is that they were hushed up in some way. Friends of Merrithew are outspoken in saying that Early got his medal today but Merrithew, who was supporting Early in the demand for recognition, is still out in the cold.
>
> It is understood that Early had Connecticut Congressional support for a medal. That counted. The War Department states that Early was the only one of the survivors recommended for a medal within the legal time limit.
>
> Everything today was serene on the surface, but that apparent serenity hid a good deal of devious maneuvering. When this correspondent first told certain Army officials of Early's threatened insurgency they called the New Haven man all sorts of names and said he had got all he deserved—nothing. Today one of these same officers admitted that he was one of those who the next day recommended a medal for Early.

> The whole understructure of this week's performance is not
> straight and frank or statesmanlike and it is a question whether the
> War Department helped itself in the long run with its expedient
> solution of the troubles.

As for the re-creation of the battle, Griffin stated that it "was noisy but
not totally convincing. . . . The original cast of that Argonne exploit hung
around the side lines this afternoon and hardly looked at the drama."[68]

The way the War Department overlooked the other survivors could not
be hidden from some of the reporters or the attendees. The department
not only deliberately led the other men to believe they would get medals
but also attempted to hide the survivors' grievances from the general public in order to protect their use of York's story and the War College Exposition. In fact, in October 1930, the US Army *Infantry Journal* published
an article about Alvin York's exploit written by Capt. Henry O. Swindler,
who organized the War College Carnival and Exposition the year prior.
The article confirms the War Department's feelings toward the other
men. Although Swindler included Merrithew's name in connection with
the War College events, he did not adjust the story to reflect Merrithew's
role. While Swindler does name the other members of the platoon and
notes that Early initially led them, he repeats the same story as previous
authors. According to Swindler, the other men "played no material part,
however, in the fight which followed, firing not more than a dozen shots
altogether." This official Army publication perpetuated the single-handed
legend and helped to establish it in the official historiography.[69] At least
in presenting the DSC to Bernard Early, the War Department officially
recognized that other men were part of the engagement. With Early
properly honored, the surviving members now had a basis to push for
their own recognition.

5

Push for Recognition

For the surviving members of the battle, the 1929 US Army War College event seemed to offer an opportunity for the recognition long due them. Even though the War Department agreed that Bernard Early deserved to be recognized, their decision to award the DSC to him alone left the other survivors disappointed. Early believed that others would be recognized, but it did not happen. Of the five who attended the War College event, Otis B. Merrithew took it the hardest. Merrithew had claimed that he, not York, was given verbal command to take over the patrol by Early, which Early confirmed.[1] However, he had not received any formal recognition or award. The unacknowledged men clearly felt slighted by the War Department. In their hope for recognition, some of the men began to turn to their senators, former commanders, and local Veterans of Foreign Wars chapters for help.

Although Early had been supported in his claim by Lt. Col. G. Edward Buxton and the American Legion in the 1920s, the other men turned elsewhere. In fact, just prior to the War College event, in late September of 1929, Selectman Philip G. Bowker of Brookline, Massachusetts, where Merrithew lived, worked with the American Legion to send letters to Massachusetts Senators David Walsh and Frederick Gillett seeking help for Merrithew's recognition.[2] Senator Walsh then opened an investigation into the acts of the other men, especially Otis Merrithew. Walsh asked the War Department for a report on Merrithew's part in the engagement to determine if he indeed deserved credit.[3] Members of the American Legion in Holyoke, Massachusetts, had also communicated with Senator Walsh in support of Joseph Kornacki, although nothing came of this effort before the War College event.[4]

After the War College exposition, Senator Walsh continued to push the case for some of the other men and told reporters that if his investigation justified it, he would seek congressional action to give awards to them. On October 6, 1929, at the conclusion of the exposition, Merrithew and Kornacki visited Senator Walsh.[5] This visit gave Merrithew the confidence to reach out to the senator again on October 15, 1929, which had been suggested by Brookline's Board of Selectmen, the American Legion, and the Veterans of Foreign Wars. Merrithew requested Walsh's "valuable influence and assistance" in getting the story properly recognized by the War Department, whose records reported that Merrithew had been severely wounded early in the engagement and was out of commission, details which were decidedly inaccurate.[6] News about Walsh's inquiry received some attention from the publicity division of the American Legion, which on November 13 they sent a letter to the Brookline, Massachusetts, Legion Post requesting information about Merrithew so that they could publish it.[7]

While these efforts were under way, on November 11, Robert Talley, a Newspaper Enterprise Association service writer, wrote an article about Alvin York's feat. Talley tracked down the other survivors in order to learn about their lives since the war's end. His nationally syndicated article provided brief descriptions of the men's lives. This was the first time that a report had been extended to all of the other survivors rather than focusing solely on York. Talley's report reveals the striking difference between York's life of rewards compared to that of the other men:

> Sergeant York is living quietly on his Tennessee farm that the grateful people of his state bought for him. Sergeant Bernard Early is now married and has two children, Charles and Bernard Jr. He lives in New Haven, Connecticut and operates a small restaurant. He waits on the tables while his pal does the cooking. For what he did that day, Early spent five months in a hospital.
>
> Corporal Otis Merrithew lives at Brookline, Massachusetts and has a job driving a truck for the state highway department. Two little daughters brighten his home, Jeanne, 17 months, and Anna, 5, and he values them more than he does his one good lung, the other wounded by gas. He enlisted and served under the name of William B. Cutting, a name he adopted when he ran away from home. Private Mario Muzzi's old wound in his shoulder does not interfere with his job as a baker at the National Biscuit Co. plant in New York City,

although it cost him two months in the hospital back in 1918. Private Percy Beardsley has gone back to his father's farm near Roxbury, Connecticut. He is the son of "Nate" Beardsley, a champion breeder of Devonshire cattle. He has never married.

Private Joseph Kornacki is a mill worker at Holyoke, Massachusetts and has two children. The whereabouts of Private Feodor Sok and Private Thomas Johnson are unknown. Private Michael Sacina, born in Italy and reared in New York. He told a reporter that since his return from the army he has had very bad luck, being out of a job quite often. He is a very small man. Recently he applied for a job as a subway guard and was turned down because he was too short. Just now he has the coat and hat checking concession in a New York barber shop.

Private Patrick Donohue is a mill worker in Lawrence, Massachusetts but has had the misfortune to be out of a job recently. He is unmarried. Private George Mills drives his feed wagon in South Philadelphia every day and not even his customers know that he is a war hero. He's had a lot of hard luck too.[8]

This article emphasized that when the battle ended, Alvin York got praise and rewards, but the lives of the "Other Sixteen" ended in obscurity due to the "single-handed" myth.

By February 9, 1930, Senator Walsh had received assurance from the War Department that it would give the matter every consideration.[9] Nevertheless, the department seems to have dropped the investigation shortly thereafter. Over a year later, Brookline Selectman Philip Bowker wrote Senator Walsh about the investigation. The senator advised Bowker that he would be glad to reopen the matter by asking the War Department about its progress.[10] Unfortunately, Senator Walsh's inquiry failed to move it forward.

Merrithew was also supported by US Representative Robert Luce of Massachusetts. Luce went directly to other members of Congress, and instead of going through the War Department, he introduced a bill "to allow the Distinguished Service Cross for service in the World War to be awarded to Merrithew." This bill was presented three times—on December 11, 1929, December 8, 1931, and March 9, 1933.[11] The bill would have authorized the award to be made by the secretary of war, notwithstanding the fact that the War Department had stopped awarding citations and honors for extraordinary service during the war.[12]

Only the first attempt made it into the Committee on Military Affairs. It read:

> Be it enacted by the Senate and House of Representatives of the United States of America in Congress assembled, that the Secretary of War be, and is hereby, authorized to confer the distinguished service cross upon Otis B. Merrithew, who served under the name of Corporal William B. Cutting, formerly of Company G, Three hundred and twenty-eighth Regiment Infantry, Eighty-second Division, United States Army, for gallantry in action on October 8, 1918, while serving in a detail commanded by Sergeants Alvin C. York and Bernard Early.
>
> Sec. 2. That this award shall be made notwithstanding the fact that the War Department ceased awarding citations and honors for extraordinary service above and beyond the call of duty during the World War on April 7, 1923.[13]

Unfortunately, the bill did not make it out of the House of Representatives.

Not one to be discouraged, Merrithew reached out to Senator Marcus A. Coolidge, also of Massachusetts, on June 5, 1933. Merrithew had worked for the senator in a machine shop years before, and his sister had looked after Coolidge's children. Merrithew had hoped that writing an old friend might better his chance of success. He wrote Coolidge that he had lost the $20 pension he had been receiving from the Veterans' Bureau, which had covered his expenses when he missed work as a result of being gassed during the war. He also added that he had sworn affidavits (which will be discussed later in the chapter) from the other survivors which proved he should be decorated. Merrithew asked if "it is possible to present another Bill to Congress" or at the least receive a Silver Star, if not the DSC. Merrithew ended the letter with "I am taking the liberty of putting this before you because I feel that if anybody can help me, you will."[14] Unfortunately, his letter went unanswered.

At the same time that he contacted his senators and congressman, Merrithew sought help from yet another influential individual. At the War College event in 1929, he met his former battalion commander, Lt. Col. G. Edward Buxton, who had helped in Early's successful effort for recognition. Merrithew spent an afternoon discussing his side of the story. During their meeting, Buxton told Merrithew that he would "do all in [his] power to get [him] the DSC."[15] Buxton later recalled this meeting to Maj. Gen. Duncan, stating that he "was able to avert a very embarrassing situation for the officers in charge of the show by getting Cutting [Merrithew] one [*sic*] side and listening to his story, examining the scars in his left arm—all flesh wounds."[16]

After the War College Exposition, Merrithew and Buxton exchanged letters about Merrithew's case, letters that would date from 1929 to 1935. Most of the correspondence between the men has not been made public until now. It shines a light on various aspects of the War Department, the official York story, and the acceptance of the role of the other men. Shortly after the end of the War College Exposition, Merrithew received his first letter from Buxton, dated October 8, 1929. Buxton said he would "try to assemble the facts of your case in a way which may be helpful in subsequently getting recognition of your participation in the exploits of October 8." Buxton also revealed the difficulties in the endeavor if "a technical interpretation is placed upon the existing law. In fact, it may be necessary to ask for an amendment to this law."[17] The law he referred to was continuation of H. R. Bill 10297, which extended the time limit for recommendations for awards until May 26, 1928.[18] Buxton also said he had written Maj. (former Capt.) Edward C. B. Danforth Jr. for comments.[19]

Buxton's next letter, dated October 18, 1929, revealed the steps necessary to get Merrithew the DSC. This letter stated the case as follows:

> In our efforts to secure a decoration for you it would seem advisable to avoid, as far as possible, purely controversial or disputed points and take the attitude that there was glory enough for all the leaders in this exploit. I have been in correspondence with Capt. Danforth and I understand that he is willing, on my recommendation, to start the ball rolling with a recommendation that you be given the Distinguished Service Cross. Upon receipt of his recommendation I will urge it with the War Department. If it is necessary to get a bill through Congress extending the time limits for initiating recommendations for decorations, I will do what I can to get such a bill introduced. After giving considerable thought to this matter I think the strongest ground upon which we can base your claims lies in the fact that although receiving five wounds in the left arm you showed great bravery and devotion to duty, continuing to participate as well as possible in the firefight which followed against overwhelming odds and that you, although wounded, assisted in evacuating the prisoners before consenting to go to the hospital.[20]

In response to this letter, Merrithew wrote a sworn statement with his side of the story and sent it out to the other survivors. He received signed and notarized signatures from Bernard Early, Feodor Sok, Patrick Donohue, and Percy Beardsley.[21]

In the next letters, dated October 28, 1929, and December 9, 1929, Buxton requested the addresses of the other survivors so that he could obtain their testimonies. Merrithew obliged. Buxton also told Merrithew that the sworn statements that he had just obtained from the other men were not sufficient due to a technical formal issue because "decorations are not given out as the result of affidavits made by the person himself, but because of statements made, as a rule, by eyewitnesses of his actions."[22] In other words, the affidavits in question were written as Merrithew's statement of facts and were sworn to by the others rather than being their first-person accounts. By February 21, 1930, Buxton had approached former Plt. Sgt. Harry Parsons about the engagement. Buxton also reiterated the fact that Congress would need to pass a bill extending the time for awarding decorations.[23]

On April 2, 1930, Buxton said that he still had not received any response from the other men. Nevertheless, he agreed to "draft an affidavit myself recommending you for the DSC, based upon your own statement that you continued in the firefight after being seriously wounded and that you assisted in bringing out the column." Buxton also revealed why he wanted to help Merrithew even though he had not witnessed the battle. "My only interest is based upon the point that I never refused to listen patiently to any man who ever served under me and have always endeavored to aid any such wherever possible."[24] Buxton was not the kind of man to pursue this issue simply to placate Merrithew. He had sincere respect for the men who served under him and would not have supported Merrithew's claims if he had not genuinely believed them. At the time, he was the president of the B.B.&R. Knight Corporation, with numerous demands on his time.

With a letter dated April 8, 1930, Buxton reached out to Gen. Charles P. Summerall, Chief of Staff, US Army. Eight days later, Buxton responded to Merrithew that he had favorable news from Summerall and would "proceed to file my own recommendation shortly in the belief that existing legislation will change and permit the subject of decorations to be reopened." He noted that both the American Legion and the Veterans of Foreign Wars had asked Congress for such an extension.[25] Buxton's letter to Summerall did have an interesting result when it was forwarded to Col. Julian R. Lindsey. As brigade commander of the 164th during the war,

Statement Of Otis B. Merrithew

Regarding Argonne Engagement

I...Patrick J. Donahue...... Do Solomly swear that the following
statement to be true and correct to the best of my knowledge.

'' On October 8'1918 in the Argonne Forest at Hill 223,
I was attached to Co. G of the 328th Infantry,82d division of A.E.F
We went over the top at approximately 6.:10 A.M. in company front.
Due to extremely heavy machine gun firing, three squads were detail
ed to silence them . The detail was under command of Sgt. Bernard
Earley.We advanced in the circumferential route to the left intend_
ing to attack the machine gun nest from the rear. We got into the
woods unnoticed and progressed along a path leading to the German
headquarters behind their second line trench when we surprised a
German medical unit. Sgt Earley commanded them to halt but they
started to run and were lost in the woods. We followed them immedia
tely to prevent them from warning of our surprise attack. Sgt
Earley distributed his men in such a way that we were very well
concealed and when finally we came upon the German headquarters,
Sgt.Earley gave the command to fire. We all opened fire at once
and in that blast fifteen to eighteen Germans fell mortally wounded
The remaining Germans got down on their knees and raised their
hands to god and cried "Kamerad: Kamerad: which we recognized as
the sign of surrender. Then Sgt. Earley said to me "this is murder
Cease firing, He gave the command to Corporal York and his squad
to keepthe Germans under cover and Sgt. Earley Corporal Cutting
and Corporal Savage and a few of our men went up to form the
prisoners in a count of two preparatory to taking them out of the
woods. While we were forming the prisoners in march formation Corp
York and his men who were still concealed, kept them under cover.
Sgt. Earley was conferring with the German Major and giving orders
to Savage and myself when all of a sudden the Germans acting under
a command in the German tongue from one of their numbers fell on
their stomachs leaving us standing. We could not quite understand
the reason for their action other than that they apparently were
unaware of our limited numbers. At the same instant that they
fell, a blast came from the machine gun nest killing six of our
men, severely wounding Sgt.Earley and slightly wounding Corporal
Cutting in the left arm. At the same instant Corporal York,
who was still concealed unknown to the Germans ,opened fire on
them. Private Beardsley ducked behind a tree and I reached my
original position and picked up fire although wounded and all of
us remaining survivors battled with the Germans for approximatle
twenty minutes Corporal York and his men were still on my right
when the Germansmachine gun firing sort of lulled or ceased.
Sgt. Earley remained with our dead on the ground in front of me
and kept calling Cutting, Cutting, if possible get me out and
take command, which I did.Firing ceased and the German Major
kept hollering We have had enough.We give up,so I gave the command
to the seven survivors to get the prisoners together and lined
up. The German Major came forward and passed me his pistol which
surrender was witnessed by all the survivors, After we got them
lined up, we still had the front German line trench to go through
which we did successfully after warning the German Major that

failure to strictly obey our orders would cost him his life. After
we left the woods, we saw at approximately 125 yards away our own
battalion command which we had advanced ahead of in the morning. In
that group, I recognized Battalion Adjutant Lt. Woods and Sgt. Parson
We proceeded to march the prisoners towards our command and they
towards us. When we met Sgt. Parsons looked at my helmet and saw
that there were three bullet holes in it. He pulled the helmet off
and said,"Cutting, you're hit.' I replied 'No, not there,'and pointed
to my arm and said 'I have a flesh wound here I think.'At that time,
he tried to pull me out of line to give me first aid. I said,'No,
To Hell with first aid,' Look at the souvenir I have. meaning the
German pistol, Sgt.Parsons recalled this incident at the recent
exposition given in Washington, October 5,1929.) He persisted in my
getting first aid and I heard Lt. Woods ask for the senior non
commissioned officer remaining, who was Corporal York. York stepped
forward and said ' I am, sir,' and then was given command, Lt. Woods
gave York besides the seven survivors four or five more men bringing
the detail up to eleven or twelve men to take the prisoners back
to divisional headquarters. As York got the prisoners headed toward
the rear of the lines, I came out of the shack where I had received
first aid. Sgt. Parsons commanded me to go to the hospital but instea
I fell in line with the detail and helped escort the prisoners back
as far as the ambulance row. We put Sgt. Earley and as I recall a
wounded German Lieutenant in the first ambulance and I hopped into
the next after bidding the fellows good bye. They then continued
on with the prisoners Affidavits from the survivors will substantiate
these facts. I was very much surprised not to have been asked for
an affidavit from York when his book was in preparation for I had
been on the platform with him at Tremont Temple in Boston. He knew
at that time that I was living in Charlestown and that my real name
was Merrithew. I have been told that Major Buxton and Sgt. Earley
tried to locate me years ago to talk the matter over. They,however,
were not aware of the fact that I had enlisted under an assumed name.
At the same time,however, I was being carried on the government
payroll as a vocational student at the U.S. Veterens Bureau in
Boston. York knows the true story which is not consistant with the
narration in his book. I would not have been so anxious to press
this claim were it not for the urging of my fellow survivors and
friends who feel that a great injustice has been done.

Signed...*Patrick E Donohue*...

Then personally appeared before me the above named *Patrick J. Donohue*
and swore that the foregoing statements were true and correct

Subscribed and sworn to before me, this 16th day of
November 1929. of Lawrence, Massachusetts
Signed...*William Mahoney*...

Notary Public

Sworn Statement of Otis B. Merrithew signed by Patrick Donohue, November 16, 1929.
Courtesy of Jimmy Fallon.

Col. Lindsey was the author of General Orders No. 1, Headquarters, 164th Brigade, 82nd Division, AEF, dated Sunday, May 4, 1919, that had awarded Silver Star citations to George Wills, Percy Beardsley, Patrick Donohue, Michael Sacina, and Joseph Kornacki, as well as General Orders No. 11 which cited Michael Sacina. After Lindsey received the letter from Buxton, he wrote the adjutant general, US Army, Washington, DC, on April 18, 1930. In his letter, Lindsey said that in light of the new information a citation should have been given to all the men of the platoon, living and deceased.[26] Unfortunately, this citation does not seem to have been made official.

Letter from General Lindsey to the Adjutant General, April 18, 1930. Courtesy of Jimmy Fallon.

Buxton's increasing interest in the roles of the other men began to affect how he handled official business in the media. On September 9, 1930, the *Providence Journal* ran an article announcing that the 82nd Division's first homecoming celebration would take place in Atlanta, Georgia, September 26 through 28. The announcement included the story of Alvin York's single-handed exploit. In response, Buxton wrote a letter to the newspaper, which was published on September 13, 1930. Buxton's letter denounced the rumor that he had ever supported the notion that York operated alone. He went on to emphasize that he did not want his name associated with any publication that ran that version of the story. He also said that "the references in this article to Sergeant York's exploit, however, were not obtained from me and, unfortunately, help to perpetuate a popular misunderstanding which is unjust to a group of Sergeant York's comrades."[27]

Buxton continued, arguing that "York did not perform his now famous enterprise 'single-handed,' nor as historian of the division have I ever supported such a statement. In the official history of the 82nd Division we set forth the story of 17 men, four non-commissioned officers, of whom York was one, and 13 privates, who in an isolated wooded ravine attacked, fought and captured 132 Germans . . . leaving some 20 of the enemy dead upon the steep hillside of that desperate battleground." Buxton concluded his letter saying that "time and ceaseless repetition have added certain mythological aspects to the story, as has probably been the case with all men whose deeds become woven with military legends. I do not wish an article to stand without comment which implies any sponsorship on my part of the 'single-handed' legend or the 'one-man army.'"[28] As Buxton learned the facts of October 8 from Otis and the other survivors, he increasingly refused to stand by a story that diminished the roles of the other men. He also continued to help Merrithew.

Unfortunately, despite the efforts of Buxton and the Senators, as well as Merrithew's persistence, the law was not changed. Over a year later, Merrithew reached out to his old commander once more. In his reply to Merrithew on May 19, 1931, Buxton said he had had no luck reaching the other men. He attached a "suggested form of recommendation for the Distinguished Service Cross" that Merrithew would need to have signed by the other men. Buxton also said that Joseph Kornacki and Percy Beardsley had responded to his inquiries and wanted to arrange times to meet.[29] Merrithew wrote to Buxton expressing the difficulties some of the men had with the lack of access to a notary and the lack of familiarity with legal documents. On May 29, 1931, Buxton replied that he could draft a statement that would not require an oath. Buxton also said that if Merrithew would return the affidavit, he would "send it to Sergeant York myself and ask him if he feels that he can conscientiously sign the same."[30]

B. B. & R. Knight Corporation

"Fruit of the Loom" and other cotton fabrics

Providence, R. I.

Office of the President

May 19th, 1931.

Corp. Otis B. Merrithew
300 Boylston Street,
Brookline, Massachusetts.

My dear Merrithew:-

              I am glad to hear from you this morning and have been refreshing my mind by examining my files containing correspondence with you, Captain Danforth and others. I assume that you're referring to the sentence in my letter of October 18th, 1929 in which I said .. "I have been in correspondence with Capt Danforth and I understand that he is willing, on my recommendation, to start the ball rolling with a recommendation that you be given the Distinguished Service Cross." This was based on a letter which I had received, dated October 11th, 1929, from Captain Danforth in answer to a letter I had written him following our meeting in Washington. He closed his letter to me with the statement "If I can help in any way further with the Cutting matter please let me know". On October 23rd, 1929, however, Captain Danforth wrote me again saying that he would prefer that I initiate the recommendation as he had no first hand knowledge of the part you played. He added that he wanted you to get the decoration if you deserved it and was willing to take my judgment in the matter and help to the extent of writing a letter to accompany the recommendation for citation, although he did not feel competent to sign the application himself knowing so little about the merits of the case. Since that time, as you know, I have written many letters to other survivors of the detachment inviting them to make statements which they would be willing to sign and which would serve as an application. This I proposed to support in any way I could in a letter stating that I had talked with you and believed the affidavits made by eye witnesses to be correct. I am sure you realize that my difficulty all along has been in the matter of eye witnesses. It seems exceedingly difficult to get any of the men with you to make frank statements. This may be due either to the fact that none of them saw much during the fight except the person on his right and left or it may be due to the fact that they feel they have something to urge in their own behalf which they wish considered first.

              I enclose, herewith, a suggested form of recommendation for the Distinguished Service Cross. I should be glad to see you

secure as many signatures as possible to this from all or part
of the following men.

Sergeant Bernard Early	13 Bishop St., New Haven, Conn.
Private Percy Beardsley	Roxbury, Connecticut.
Private Joseph Konotski	7 Plymouth Place, Holyoke, Mass.
Private Michael Sacina	654 East 156 St., New York City.
Private George W. Wills	2307 Stone House Villa, Philadelphia
	Penna.
Private Patrick Donahue	21 Cooke Street, Lawrence, Mass.
Private Feodor Sok	13 Bradford St, Ashley, Penna.

The last addresses which we have in this office are those which I have
given above against the names. In the case of Sacina and Wills, I sent
my letters to them by registered mail - received the return card but no
answer. Donahue's registered letter was returned to us. I heard nothing
from Johnson. Konotski wrote suggesting that we talk together sometime,
but I have not been able to go to Holyoke and he has not been able to
come down here. The same is true with Beardsley who lives over in
Connecticut. If the enclosed affidavit is signed by as many of the
survivors as possible and sent to me, I will forward it to General
Lindsey and ask him and General Duncan to write letters to accompany
the application to the War Department. So far as I know the law is
unchanged which shuts out awards not already recommended in the files
of the War Department. That, however, is a matter by itself and might
be changed anytime by Congress. I have felt myself about at the end of
my rope in this matter without the frank, whole-hearted cooperation of
the other men in the detachment.

        With best wishes,

                        Sincerely yours,

GEB.H
                        G. Edward Buxton.

Letter from G.E. Buxton to Otis Merrithew, May 19, 1931. Courtesy of Jimmy Fallon.

By June, Merrithew was still obtaining signatures from the other men.
On June 11, 1931, Buxton wrote that sending the affidavits out individ-
ually would work but that it would be best to have all the men sign one
document so that "a man who is a little doubtful" could see "the other
names ahead of his," which would make any doubters "feel that he is acting with a group rather than alone." He then reiterated that if Merrithew
would send him the affidavit, he would "send one to Sergeant York with
a personal note from me. I do not, of course, know what he will say, but
I think there might be a better chance of obtaining his help if the letter
came from me."[31]

Merrithew wrote to the other men and sent them the recommendation written by Buxton. Early, Beardsley, Donohue, and Sok, all signed, and had the statements notarized before returning them to Merrithew. He then sent the statements to Buxton. On June 27, 1931, Buxton wrote to congratulate Merrithew on securing the sworn statements from the

I, *Percy P. Beardsley* (address) *Roxbury* ......(rank). *Mechanic*
formerly member of Company G, 328th Infantry 82nd Division, A. E. F.
being duly sworn do hereby state and affirm as follows:

I was a member of the detachment of three squads from Company G.,
Second Battalion 328th Infantry commanded by Sergeant Bernard Early which
executed a surprise attack upon a German machine gun battalion in the
meuse Argonne offensive a little northwest of Chatel-Chehery on October
8th, I918. The other non commissioned officers with this platoon were
Acting Corporal Alvin C, York, Acting Corporal Otis B. Merrithew
(enlisted William B, Cutting) and Corporal Murray Savage After we had
surprised a part of the enemy force and secured its surrender we received
a heavy fire from other elements of the enemy battalion located on the
hillside above us. Acting Corporal Savage was killed. Acting Corporal Yorks
contribution to the victorious fire fight whic followed is well known and
has been given deserved recognition The Distinguished Service Cross has
benn appropiatley awarded to Sergeant Bernard Early. The undersigned
hereby recomend that the Distinguished Service Cross be awarded Acting
Corporal Otis B, Merrithew of 300 Boylston Street, Brookline Massachusetts,
for his personal conduct and contribution to the leadership of the
detachment,s exploit In the early stage of the fire fight Acting Corporal
Merrithew received five bullets in the left arm. Notwithstanding these
wounds he continued with great bravery and devotion to duty to participate
in the fire fight which followed against overwhelming numbers of the enemy
Upon the surrender of the enemy Acting Corporal Merrithew (Cutting)
in spite of his wounds assisted in the evacuation of I32 prisoners before
permitting himself to be sent to the hospital.

Sign. *Percy P. Beardsley*

County of *Litchfield*

State *Connecticut*

Then personally appeared before me the above named *Percy P. Beardsley*
and swore that the foregoing statements to be true and correct........
this *19* Day of *June* 1931: at *Roxbury*

Nomos H. Murllot Justice of Peace
Notary Public

Sworn Affidavit of Percy Beardsley, June 19, 1931. Courtesy of Jimmy Fallon.

other men. He also said that he had written to York but had not received
an answer. Nevertheless, with the sworn statements Buxton would "send
along what we have with a suitable letter to Col. [Julian R.] Lindsey asking him, in turn, to forward with an endorsement to General [George
B.] Duncan, requesting the latter to send with his own comments to the
War Department." Buxton concluded by saying that he had been told
that a bill to extend the period for the award of medals would probably
be proposed and be passed in Congress.[32]

Almost a year later, Merrithew checked in with Buxton again. On
March 3, 1932, Buxton's secretary replied that he had never received an
affidavit from Sgt. York. However, Buxton did send all the others with a
strong personal recommendation to Gen. Lindsey.[33] Buxton also sent a
letter to Maj. Gen. Duncan on April 22, 1932, in order to ascertain his
opinion on the matter. In this letter, Buxton revealed many of his personal
beliefs regarding Merrithew's case. Buxton confessed he had "taken an
additional interest in this whole matter in order to silence some of the
efforts to discredit Sergeant York." He believed that Early was responsible for the successful attack and that York won the firefight. Buxton told
Duncan that they "would have been justified in giving Division Citations
to every member of the little party." However, Buxton saw that the men
were sincere in their support of Merrithew's claim and stated that York
had admitted he "didn't know what anybody in the detachment did except
himself." Buxton sought to make certain the situation with Merrithew
would be "settled right before we drop it forever." [34] (See appendix 1.)

While awaiting news about the case, Merrithew applied for and
received his Purple Heart medal on June 27, 1932, for "wound received
in action on October 8, 1918 while serving as a Pvt., with Company
G, 328th Infantry."[35] On October 24, 1932, Merrithew received news
from Lt. Col. Buxton, who forwarded a copy of the letter Gen. Lindsey
had sent to the adjutant general in 1930. Buxton stated that Merrithew
should ask for his Silver Star on the strength of this recommendation
because the law still blocked the awarding of the DSC. However, Buxton
also told Merrithew that were there any Act of Congress to extend the
recommendation period, he would be glad to revive Merrithew's application to receive the DSC. In the meantime, Buxton agreed to forward
the affidavits in his possession to Maj. Gen. Duncan and ask him to get
the matter on record in the War Department.[36]

On December 29, 1932, Buxton's secretary sent Merrithew a copy of the War Department's acknowledgment to Maj. Gen. Duncan that it had received the recommendation and papers filed by Lt. Col. Buxton on Merrithew's behalf.[37] This was a hopeful sign; maybe Merrithew would finally receive some recognition. On his end, Merrithew followed up with the War Department about his Silver Star recommendation from Gen. Lindsey. On November 2, 1933, Merrithew received a reply from US Army Adj. Gen. James McKinley, who said that "no record has been found to show that you were awarded any citation for gallantry in action in any orders . . . therefore it is regretted that your application for the Silver Star decoration cannot receive favorable consideration."[38]

While these events transpired, other survivors began to express their feelings about the matter. Feodor Sok wrote Lt. Col. Danforth on May 16, 1933, expressing his displeasure with York. "It's a shame us boys, we done the whole job and one man got credit for what the whole bunch of us done."[39] Sok also "boldly wrote to the Government" about receiving his due credit. He received the reply "We find you have no claims to any compensation."[40] Merrithew also received a letter from William S. Payton, who had also served in Company G, 328th Infantry, 82nd Division, during the war. Payton wrote the letter mainly to catch up with Merrithew, but he also revealed his feelings toward Alvin York. "I cut a clipping from the *Brockton Enterprise* the other night. It's a picture of an old friend of yours, Alvin C. York. You'll notice this John Hix that puts these pictures in the paper every night said he [York] captured the Germans *almost* single handed. York still seems to be creating a lot of publicity every now and then. Don't think because I said he was an old friend of yours that I really meant it. You know what I think of him. I don't want to waste any more time talking about that guy."[41]

Ever persistent, Merrithew once again wrote a letter to Senator Marcus Coolidge on April 24, 1935. In his letter, Merrithew said that over the last few years he had been recommended for the DSC several times for the part he played in the battle. He asked the Senator if there was any bill pending before Congress to repeal the law preventing him from receiving the DSC that Buxton recommended him for.[42] Coolidge replied that he had taken the case "up with the War Department here, and they have informed me that no legislation will be accepted by them at this time regarding your case. It is quite possible that later the War Department may recommend legislation which will give you the honor and merit which you deserve."[43] With that response, Merrithew's chances of being recognized slipped away. As this record makes clear, the only reason Merrithew did not receive either the Silver Star or a DSC was the time limit that the federal law put on awards.

As Merrithew's hopes for recognition faded, a new avenue opened for Bernard Early. The American Legion, Department of Connecticut, held its state convention August 8–10, 1935. At the conference, New Haven Post No. 47 presented a resolution that stated in part:

> Whereas, that the Second District of the American Legion, Depart-ment of Connecticut goes on record as a favor of a review of facts, by the War Department, or if necessary by Congressional action, the case of Bernard Early for an award of the Congressional Medal of Honor, for his leadership of a detachment of men from Company 'G,' 328th Inf. As acting Sargeant [sic] it is he who led the men which made the capture of a large body of Germans, and WHEREAS, that the American Legion, Department of Connecticut, favors a true and im-partial hearing on all facts of the acts performed by this detachment of men in action at Chatel-Chéhéry, France, on October 8, 1918, and WHEREAS, at this time the credit of the entire capture is given to one man.[44]

This resolution passed unanimously. Immediately following the con-vention, the story became national news.

As newspapers spread the information, commentators began to char-acterize the story as a fight between Early and Alvin York. When asked to comment about the Connecticut American Legion's resolution, York's only comment was "all this is old news."[45] Reporters pulled records from the 1929 War College exposition stating that "Army records show that the board of military officers which reviewed Early's service record and rec-ommended the award of the Distinguished Service Cross had considered awarding him the Medal of Honor but finally decided that the award of the DSC, the second highest recognition for valor in the American army, would be sufficient recognition."[46]

Even Early's physician in New Haven, Dr. Frank Mongillo, was inter-viewed as part of this story. Dr. Mongillo revealed that Early was "very modest, extremely cheerful, and very reluctant about discussing the war." He also said that Early was "suffering from a severe wound in his spine caused by gun shot and from a heart condition. He is very nervous."

Finally, he concluded that it was a well-known fact among the other survivors that Early should have been credited for being in charge of the patrol instead of York, which had been righted at the War College Carnival and Exposition.[47] Lt. Col. Edward C. B. Danforth Jr. also commented on the American Legion's resolution, calling it "entirely unwarranted." Danforth said he was not disparaging Early, but when he personally investigated the circumstances, "credit was given where credit was due" because Early had gone down before "the real fight started."[48] This argument captured the country's attention and was even broadcast on the radio.

The broadcast about the Legion's resolution reached a fellow World War I veteran named Elijah L. Ellis of Experiment, Georgia. Ellis had served as a private in Company G, 328th Infantry, 82nd Division, during the war. When the survivors exited the woods with the German prisoners on October 8, 1918, Ellis helped Early onto a stretcher and assisted in carrying him until he was loaded onto an ambulance. Ellis said that Early "certainly deserves more credit than anyone else."[49] Though touching, this affirmation of Early's role did little to further the case. and no legislation to award Early the Medal of Honor was ever presented to Congress. However, Connecticut Representative James Andrew Shanley presented a bill in the House of Representatives on November 17, 1937, "authorizing the President of the United States to appoint Corp. Bernard Early as a major in the United States Army and then place him on the retired list."[50] This would have given Early a pension and some distinction, but the bill did not make it out of the House.

The 1930s had given the men many chances to finally receive recognition or even greater awards, but every opportunity fell through. The nation was not moved by the survivors' quest for recognition. Alvin York remained on his pedestal as the world moved toward another world war. The short-lived magazine *Ken* presented the best eulogy for Merrithew's and Early's attempts to bring some attention to the other men as well as the control of York's story by other parties. On April 21, 1938, journalist Barron C. Watson published an article, "The Men Who Helped a Hero," based on an interview with Percy Beardsley. The beginning of the article reads:

> It wasn't Sergeant York himself, it was the mass-momentum of the war-time propaganda machine and the hot air of political windbags, that blew up his truly remarkable exploit to the proportions of a pipe

dream. So the publicity ignored, and the public forgot, the sixteen men who were with the war's greatest hero, that day he "singlehanded" captured those 132 Germans.[51]

The article then detailed the encounter with Beardsley and retold the battle of October 8, 1918, reiterating the common thread of the story that the Other Sixteen, those not recognized, "got nothing except whatever German bullets they accumulated as souvenirs."[52] The article ended with a list of all the members of the platoon.

Twenty years had passed since the firefight at Chatel-Chéhéry, and the survivors had now exhausted all avenues that would have given them recognition. National news, congressional intervention, assistance from commanding officers, radio broadcasts—none of these options were able to break through the legend of Sgt. Alvin York. The men fell from public memory as York continued to be revered as America's "greatest hero," while in Europe and in the Far East, Nazi Germany and Imperial Japan began making aggressive moves that would ultimately take the United States into another world war. Plans made on the other side of the world would have a profound impact on the story of these men and put them in the public spotlight in a way they could never have imagined.

6

The World Is Quick to Forget

By 1939, the sixteen survivors were largely forgotten, as were their efforts for recognition over the last decade. And so the men fell from public memory. Americans struggled through the Great Depression, political turmoil, and social displacement, none of which created an ideal environment for military recognition of the "Other Sixteen." On September 1, 1939, Nazi Germany invaded Poland, starting another world war, which would last for the next six years. Recalling the horrors of World War I and the failure of the Treaty of Versailles, American isolationists responded to the war in Europe by reinforcing their idea that their country should not intervene in foreign affairs. Alvin C. York was prominent among these isolationists, preaching against intervention in another European war.

As Hitler's power grew in Europe, the American people struggled to decide what role they should play. Several Hollywood studios worked to ensure that Americans were informed about the dangers of Hitler's regime. Warner Bros. which was led by the Polish-born, Jewish brothers Harry and Jack Warner, was particularly sensitive to the topic and produced several antifascist and pro-intervention films from the mid-1930s to the early 1940s.[1] The most influential of these films would be *Sergeant York*, which premiered in 1941. The film used the "greatest hero of World War I" as a symbol of America and urged Americans to cast off their isolationist views and support a war that would create a safer future.

The film eventually grossed nearly $4 million, which made it the top movie of 1941.[2] Movie idol Gary Cooper played Alvin C. York, following his story from hell-raiser to devout Christian and from conscientious objector to soldier. Cooper won the Academy Award for Best Actor for his portrayal of York. In addition, *Sergeant York* won Oscars for Best

Film Editing and was nominated for nine other categories, including Best Picture.[3] Today the American Film Institute ranks *Sergeant York* as number 57 on its list of the 100 most inspiring films of all time.[4] In 2008 the National Film Registry added the movie to their list for being "culturally, historically, or aesthetically significant."[5]

The popularity of the movie would effectively end the other survivors' hope to be part of the battle's legacy. The film took the legend created by Duncan and early authors and solidified a new myth surrounding Alvin York as a person and his role in the engagement on October 8, 1918.[6] To make the movie, the studio required releases from the other survivors, which it eventually acquired albeit through exploitative tactics, leaving these heroes with little other than a small token compensation. When these men, led by Otis Merrithew, spoke out against this treatment and tried to get representation for their role, the studio and the media reported their stories in an utterly insulting way, belittling them and making their voices as insignificant as possible. The newspapers portrayed them as jealous comrades who only wanted to cash in on Alvin York's fame. Unfortunately, as will be discussed in detail later, this view is alive today in the work of authors such as Douglass Mastriano and James Carl Nelson.

Jesse L. Lasky, a producer for Warner Bros. had witnessed York's reception in New York City when he returned from France in May 1919. Inspired by York's story, throughout the 1930s, Lasky persistently pursued the idea of making a film. But York refused, reportedly because of his religious objections to movies and his isolationist views. Now with another war breaking out in Europe, Lasky had an even greater incentive to make York's life into a movie that would encourage the American people to act. Lasky and Harry Warner eventually convinced York to transform from pacifist to interventionist and agree to a film about himself, even if York originally wanted the film to focus on his religious conversion rather than the military side of his story.[7] However, Hollywood, like York's commanders, early authors, and the US Army, wanted to use York's story for their own goals.

For an isolationist, Christian America, York symbolized a God-fearing man who was moved to action when sufficiently provoked for the better good of the world. The film was to celebrate the religio-patriotic nature of York's story, just as George Pattullo had done in 1919.[8] On March 24, 1940, York signed a contract with Warner Bros. for a movie based on his life. He was paid $50,000 and promised 2 percent of the box-office gross. He was also given full editorial control over the screenplay. If the film demeaned, insulted, or antagonized him in any significant way, the contract permitted him to withdraw his support.[9] This meant that the studio had to play carefully to York, who had considerable power over the film's portrayal of events.

The studio immediately set to work on a script for the film, starting with several books about his life. By 1940, at least three books had told York's story. The first, *Sergeant York and His People* by Samuel K. Cowan, published in 1922, focused on York's prewar life in Appalachia, while including the story of his military exploits. The second and third books, respectively, *Sergeant York: His Own Life Story and War Diary* (1928) and *Sergeant York: Last of the Long Hunters* (1930), were both written by Thomas John Skeyhill.

Warner Bros. writers began with Cowan, whose contract with York did not specifically define who owned the movie rights of the story. Attorneys for Warner Bros. John S. Hale and Walter L. Bruington discussed the details in a letter dated June 3, 1940. Hale said plainly "I do not think that Warner Brothers will want to base the motion picture on this book. It is the least reliable of the three books which have been written about the Sergeant."[10] Nevertheless, they made some sort of agreement with Cowan because they reprinted his book with a dust jacket featuring Gary Cooper as Alvin York. Ultimately, Skeyhill's books and their version of York's story were cited as the basis for the movie.

When he heard that the movie was in production, Otis Merrithew preemptively sent a letter directly to Jesse Lasky on June 12, 1940, asking if the studio planned to include the other survivors. Merrithew wrote:

> I have contacted all of York's and my former "buddies" and they claim that they did not sign any affidavits and if they signed any papers in France they thought that they were signing a "supply slip" for a suit of underwear or some other thing. These same men today *will* sign an affidavit and forward it to the United Press if you proceed to go through with any battle scenes without consulting us six survivors.
>
> It is time that the good Sergeant thought more of the six eyewitnesses than he does, and we think that we should have prominent parts in the picture also. There is glory enough to go all the way around and it seems very ridiculous to the people of New England and all veterans that one man could do all that York claimed he did.[11]

Merrithew suggested that the picture would not do so well in New England, where most of the other survivors came from; with all but Johnson in nearby states. He warned that the bad press created by neglecting these men would hurt the studio's investment. Finally, Merrithew attached the sworn statement that the other survivors had signed ten years before and offered to provide the studio with the men's names and addresses.

Somewhat reminiscent of the prelude to the War College event nearly a dozen years earlier, this letter set off a chain of communications as the studio tried to decide how to move forward with the movie. The script, which had already been started, continued to change with more focus on the battle. This required the permission of the survivors if they were to be portrayed. Lasky sent the letter to Roy Obringer, head of the Warner Bros. legal department, for consideration on how to proceed.[12] Attorneys got involved to determine the legal ramifications of ignoring Merrithew's claims. After reading the letter and speaking with Alvin York, John S. Hale wrote to Walter Bruington on July 29, 1940, saying that "nowhere in the Congressional Record, in any of the books about Sergeant [York], nor in any of the reports of the battle, in so far as I know, has there ever been one word which casts any reflection on the parts played by the other survivors."[13]

Hale also stated: "I think there is nothing whatever to Corporal Cutting's [Merrithew's] letter, and that he cannot now go back on what he has formerly sworn and cast his sworn statement aside by merely saying he thought at the time he was signing a 'supply slip' for a suit of underwear. His letter is merely a demand for a little 'hush' money which should receive no consideration whatsoever."[14] Contrary to Hale's assertion, Merrithew had never even been approached for, much less provided, a sworn statement at the time of York's Medal of Honor investigation, even though he was still in France recovering from his wounds. Moreover, if Hale did indeed go to York for confirmation as asserted, why did York not mention the 1929 War College event where Bernard Early had been awarded his Distinguished Service Cross of which Hale seemed to be ignorant.

The issue of recognizing the other men continued to haunt the studio as they dealt with other details such as copyrights and finalizing Gary Cooper's contract. On August 27, 1940, Roy Obringer wrote to Morris Ebenstein to ask if they could proceed with filming the battle as historically accurate and reenact it in film using the names of the other men without fear of libel or privacy claims. Obringer noted that Merrithew's letter is "nothing but a peeve . . . with a hope of some monetary return." Jesse Lasky, Morris Ebenstein, and Roy Obringer soon met to discuss the risks of ignoring Merrithew and the other survivors.

In a letter from September 11, 1940, to Jacob Wilk, Obringer discusses their decision. He said Merrithew's June 12 letter "shows Cutting [Merrithew] as having a very belligerent attitude toward York and seems to be an effort on the part of Cutting [Merrithew] to take some of the bows for the feat accredited to York." Obringer said the letter had no importance beyond indicating that the other survivors might be difficult to deal with. Lasky must delete certain scenes or obtain releases from the men to use their identities in the film. Obringer listed the names of the men and said that they must track them down in order to secure the releases.[15]

To accomplish this daunting task of collecting the releases from all the survivors and others who were to be portrayed in the film, the studio chose Bill Guthrie, who had worked for the Federal Bureau of Investigation (FBI) before joining Warner Bros. Guthrie's connections had made him invaluable and earned him a promotion to location manager.[16] Guthrie quickly obtained the releases from the participants in bigger roles, such as John Pershing, G. E. Buxton, and J. R. Lindsey, who agreed by early October 1940. On October 16, Guthrie met Otis Merrithew at his house.

Things went smoothly between the two men and for a while thereafter. Guthrie made a favorable impression on Merrithew and his family, especially Merrithew's daughters who enjoyed Guthrie's stories about Hollywood and the world beyond their home. After this visit, he would send the girls gifts from his travels and signed his letters to the Merrithew family with "Uncle Bill." Guthrie sent Merrithew's wife matchbooks for her collection and sent Warner Bros. publicity photos of movie stars to the children.[17] However, the initial friendly relationship between Guthrie and the Merrithew family fell victim to the completion of Guthrie's mission.

Guthrie's assignment was to acquire the signatures of the living survivors for a small or no payment so that the studio could proceed with the movie. However, when he visited Lt. Col. Edward C. B. Danforth, on October 10, 1940, Danforth demanded the exorbitant sum of $1,500 to be portrayed in the movie and Guthrie agreed.[18] Danforth received this large sum even though he was not personally present during the time of the engagement, nor was he an eyewitness to what actually transpired there that morning. By comparison, the actual survivors who had been present, had in some cases been wounded, and whose roles during the engagement had been officially acknowledged by the War Department, received pittances—sums 6 to 300 times less for their signatures.

On October 16, 1940, Merrithew discussed his role in the battle and the subsequent lack of recognition with Guthrie. Eventually, and very reluctantly, however, Merrithew signed a release for $250 agreeing to let Warner Bros. use his name and physical likeness in all facets of the film.[19] Despite no written commitment, Merrithew hoped his and the other survivor's roles would be accurately portrayed.[20] From Merrithew, Bill Guthrie moved on to find the other survivors.

Before entering into the details of the circumstances and problems with Guthrie's location of the others, it is worth considering what the men were initially paid for their releases.

Edward Danforth—$1,500

Otis Merrithew—$250

Percy Beardsley—$50

Bernard Early—$50

Joseph Kornacki—$20

Mario Muzzi—$20

Michael Sacina—$20

George Wills—$20

Feodor Sok—$20

Thomas Johnson—$10

Patrick Donohue—$5

The most shocking amount on this list is that for Donohue, an actual participant in the engagement and eventual recipient of both the Silver Star and Purple Heart. He initially received 300 times less than Danforth, a man who did not even physically participate in the engagement.[21]

Guthrie managed to pay such low sums by taking advantage of the men's financial situations. This and the difference in payments quickly became clear to the other survivors as they communicated with each other about the movie. As they discovered these discrepancies, Merrithew became the voice for the survivors, or as Warner Bros. called him the "principal beefer."[22] He continually communicated with Bill Guthrie and directly to Jesse Lasky through the next eleven months.

Beginning in November 1940, Merrithew began following up on promises Guthrie had made. Among them was that Merrithew's daughters would go to Los Angeles if the movie premiered there. Guthrie responded that he had made no such promise and that the premiere might not happen due to war conditions.[23] Merrithew sent a letter reiterating that he expected the movie to give recognition to all the survivors. If Guthrie did not insure this recognition, Merrithew claimed that he had a recording of their conversation from October 16 that would prove Guthrie had promised to do so.[24]

Merrithew then sent another stern letter to Guthrie after he learned how poorly the other survivors had been paid and how Patrick Donohue, in particular, had been exploited. In this letter, he took Guthrie to task for paying Donohue so little. "I suppose you bought him off for a couple of beers."[25] Donohue, it should be noted, suffered greatly from the war. He had been only slightly wounded on October 8, 1918, but the war followed him home. It appears that he suffered from shell shock, or what is now known as posttraumatic stress disorder (PTSD), and he may have tried to cope by turning to alcohol. Guthrie claimed that he found Donohue after spending five hours searching "the worst dives in the world. He was very under the influence of liquor and in one of the worst dives I was ever in." Guthrie claimed that he had not paid Donohue $250 because he "was told by his friends that if I gave him much money, he would be in jail before night . . . I gave Donohue $10 and he was tickled to death to get it."[26] This statement contradicts the official document, which showed the payment as $5.[27]

Incredibly, in his December 10, 1940, letter to Merrithew, Guthrie said that he had enough $250 checks to pay all the survivors, yet he did not pay them because they had not asked. He told Merrithew that had they been paying for the releases according to the "worth" of the men, with Merrithew deserving the largest payment. Guthrie also said he would still like to be friends and stay "level" with Merrithew.[28] While Merrithew's response has not survived, it appears that he did not press the matter further because in subsequent correspondence Guthrie mentioned that he felt much better knowing things were alright.[29]

In his December 26 response, Guthrie revealed that he believed several of the survivors were being "taken care of" by the legal department. However, it seems that none of the men received any additional money at that time. Only Percy Beardsley, after speaking with Merrithew, caused enough of a stir with Warner Bros that they paid him another $200.[30] Guthrie also brought up the idea of having Merrithew come to the studio to do technical work on the film because York would not do it. He told Merrithew to send a letter with the amount he wanted to be paid for this work, adding that pay for this kind of consulting was normally $100 per week plus expenses. Guthrie concluded by saying " . . . I would be tickled to death to see you here."[31] However, Merrithew did not receive the job after his response. Warner Bros. did not want Merrithew on the set as it would upset Alvin York.

By the end of the year, Merrithew had written to Joseph Kornacki about the sum he and the others had received. The two men agreed that they should work together with the other survivors to ensure that they all received a fair payment for their roles. Percy Beardsley seems to be the only man who did not want to push the case. In a letter dated January 18, 1941, Kornacki mentioned that he did not blame Beardsley for taking the money: "he must have needed the money pretty badly to sell us out but if we stick together, I'm sure we can raise the ante." Kornacki said that if the men could get organized, they could request a flat sum from Warner Bros. " . . . I believe we are worth more than a measly $250."[32]

Kornacki's January 18 letter came after the news of the releases had been reported in newspapers across the country, which put the men's names in the national spotlight once again. Frederick C. Othman wrote the original syndicated article. Newspapers all over the country picked it up and published the story, making changes and adding their own variations, including changes in the headlines. For the most part, media coverage said the ten survivors would be recognized for heroism "never accorded them in their army days."[33] But they also presented a poor image of the men and confused the reality of their situations. Headlines such as "Heroism Pays Dividends to Farmers, Bum, Truck Driver, Dump Dweller, and Waiter" and "Scout Digs Up York's Buddies" demeaned the men and portrayed them in a poor light.[34]

December 26, 1940

My dear Folks:

Otis, I will devote the first paragraph of this letter to you. It made my heart feel mighty good to get your letter and know that everything was alright, and that you saw the situation the same as I do. As for your first letter, it has been burned up and that is water over the dam, and all is as it should be.

For your information, I understand that several of the boys have been taken care of since I received your letter. Just how many and what amount they received, I do not know, as the Legal Department is now handling the situation and all I can do is recommend. Whether my recommendations will be carried out or not, I do not know. Anyway, I returned from the east on Christmas eve, and after having been gone over a week, I am a little bit rusty on the matter.

When I returned I had a long talk with Jesse Lasky and do not get too highly enthused now, because the following is only a probability. I understand that York is not coming here to do the technical work on the picture and I recommended to Mr. Lasky that you be employed to do this work if you could get away from your home long enough to do so.

You know, Otis, it costs a lot of money to bring a man from Boston to Los Angeles and return and pay all expenses, etc., and at the present time I see no way for you to bring your family with you on this trip. However, as stated before, if a world premiere of the picture is held, that may be a different story.

Now, on receipt of this I would like to have you send me an airmail letter, stating just how much money you will want to come and do the technical work on the picture. For your information and guidance, and please keep this confidential, the usual price paid for this kind of work is $100.00 per week and all expenses. Now keep this confidentially between you and I. You would probably be here six or eight weeks, and to say that I would be tickled to death to see you here is putting it lightly.

Now for Mrs. Merrithew and the girls: I received your cards yesterday, and owing to the fact that my Christmas list was made up two months ago, none was sent to you, but rest assured that Mrs. Guthrie and I appreciate them more than I can tell you. Girls, your cards were certainly sweet and I was tickled to death to get them. I am sending a man downtown today to take care of shipping something to you. Just when it will get there I can not say, but I do hope that you will think kindly of Mrs. Guthrie and I while you are enjoying it.

Santa Claus was real good to us this year, but as stated above your cards topped everything. You know, I do not know whether you realize it or not, but I think a lot of your little family, and only hope that some day we will be able to see more of each other. I know that the good Lord can not help but be good to you all and that he will bless you all with the most happy and prosperous New Year you have ever had. Anyway, my sincerest wish is just that.

Girls, we will keep sending the matches and if there are any more pictures that you would like to have, just write and let me know. I appreciate your letters so much.

With love to all of you and again a very, very happy New Year,

Sincerely yours,

WM. L. GUTHRIE

Mr. Otis Merrithew
17 Whitney Street
Chestnut Hill, Mass.

Letter from William Guthrie to Otis Merrithew, December 26, 1940.
Courtesy of Jimmy Fallon.

Various newspapers repeated the same details about what the men were doing when Guthrie found them.[35]

Percy Beardsley was a bachelor living with his father on a well-kept farm in Roxbury, Connecticut. Upon sealing the deal with Bill Guthrie, he took a swig of apple jack.[36] In Brookline, Massachusetts, Otis Merrithew, a city truck driver, lived comfortably with his wife and three daughters. He accepted the $250 so that his eldest daughter could attend at least one year of college, a dream she had almost given up.[37] Patrick Donohue was found in a nameless neighboring town. However, the articles call him George Spelvin, which they justified by saying "it isn't fair to call a hero a drunk and a bum, even though that is what he has become." The articles also claimed that Merrithew worked out a deal to give Donohue $10 a week for his balance of $250.[38] However, Donohue did not receive more than $5 until lawyers became involved. Joseph Kornacki, who lived in Holyoke, Massachusetts with his six children and worked as a mill worker was overjoyed at the windfall. Bernard Early was waiting tables at a bar in Hamden, Connecticut. Mario Muzzi was a night watchman at a paper mill in New York City, and Michael Sacina worked as a barber shop porter nearby.[39] In Philadelphia, George Wills lived near the city dump. He kept goats and made a living by salvaging tin foil, bits of brass, and old papers from a nearby smoking pile, which netted him around $5 a week. Feodor Sok was found in a veterans' Civilian Conservation Corps (CCC) camp at Buffalo, New York. Finally, Thomas Johnson was found living alone in a one-bedroom house. He had the room partitioned with a cloth and didn't show his face. He just signed the release and Guthrie left.[40]

These were the images the American public were given of the survivors. In contrast to Alvin York who had accomplished much after the war—largely through the many honors, awards, and recognition bestowed upon him—the other survivors seemed to be barely getting by.

But the reality was a bit different from what appeared in the local papers that picked up the nationally syndicated news story. Bernard Early actually *owned* the bar. Likewise, Michael Sacina owned and operated the tobacco concession in the International Magazine Barber shop. In addition to these false images of the men's employment, some of the articles actually gave York credit for starting this search. *The Ogden Standard-Examiner* said that "York, who shot down 25 Germans and made possible the capture of 132 more, asked that his comrades receive credit for their share in putting an entire German machine gun battalion out of action."[41] The reality of course, was that Merrithew set the search in motion.

The biggest issue here is that the newspaper articles reported that each man had received $250 for the use of his name. This news caused quite a stir among the survivors who had not been told about how much the others had received. On January 11, 1941, the *Philadelphia Inquirer* sought out George Wills for an interview about the releases the survivors had signed. The paper began by mentioning the men at the battle on October 8, 1918, and said that "one of them was Alvin C. York of Tennessee. The other six with him were heroes, too. But the world is quick to forget." In the interview, Wills said he did not think he would go see the film. He stated plainly that "York likes publicity too much. . . . York's been getting the credit ever since. The rest of us—we didn't get nothin." Wills told reporters that it was a myth that he was given $250, saying that he only received "20 bucks and they took the papers I signed and went away. They told me they gave the rest of the guys $10." Wills also addressed the bit about him only making $5 a week by pulling out a healthy roll of bills.[42]

Similarly, on January 16, 1941, the *Denison Herald* tracked down Thomas Johnson for an interview about his service and reaction to the film. They found "a nerve-shaken veteran" who had been "swallowed in the obscurity of a cramped second-hand magazine stand" in Denison, Texas. Johnson told the reporters that he had spoken to a Warner Bros. representative and would "be willing to go to Hollywood to take part in the picture." Despite not wanting to talk about the October 8, 1918, engagement, he admitted that the other survivors "saw plenty of action."[43]

The various newspaper reports prompted Guthrie to write Merrithew. In a letter dated January 17, 1941, Guthrie claimed he knew nothing about the publicity and did not provide any of the information himself. Had he known, he would have stopped it because the publicity departments "exaggerate things to the fullest extent." Guthrie said that once he read the part about Donohue, he immediately started the ball rolling on paying Donohue the rest of the money so that no one would think he had taken the balance of $245. Guthrie also said that he had received a letter from Joseph Kornacki and wanted to know how he should proceed. Guthrie said that Kornacki "did not take anywhere near as prominent a part in the battle as you did. However, I want to see him treated as he should be treated, and I am going to do everything in my power to get him more money, but how much do you think we should pay him?" He commented on Kornacki's financial situation: "I feel sorry for him after seeing the condition that existed in his home."[44]

The press coverage increased Merrithew's frustration about the fact that the other men were not being paid or given their due. He wrote a letter to Guthrie on March 11, 1941, that mirrored his original letter from June 12, 1940, in which he threatened to sue the studio if the men were not properly portrayed or the battle scene was not correct. He also insisted the other survivors had not signed those affidavits. Merrithew challenged York: "Why doesn't York come out with the true story and give the boys the right recognition that is due them?"[45]

Merrithew also took issue with the fact that he was not being used as a technical consultant for the film. One of the screenwriters, Abem Finkle, commented on the idea of Merrithew providing technical input:

> I heard it rumored that somebody got the bright idea to bring out a Corporal Cutting [Merrithew]. . . . to act as a tech on the picture. That would really be dynamite! As I understand it Cutting [Merrithew] is the guy who claims that York hogged all the credit unjustifiably. While he admits that York did most of the shooting, he maintains that he and some of the others helped. He also insists that it was he, not York, that brought the prisoners back and that York pulled a fast one on him by bringing in these prisoners while Cutting [Merrithew] was asleep in a shell hole. . . . I doubt if you could think of anything that could antagonize York more than to let Cutting [Merrithew] anywhere near here.[46]

Finkle's words show not only that those involved in the filming knew of the other survivors' claims and did not want the men near the film, but also that they were completely ignorant of their side of the story. There was never any mention of Merrithew sleeping in a shell hole while York turned in the prisoners. The letter also showed that the studio kept the men away in order to appease York. Guthrie addressed this problem with Merrithew in a letter written on March 18, 1941, saying "I perfectly agree with you when you say that Mr. Lasky is making a mistake by not having you here to help with the battle sequences of the picture."[47]

In the same letter, Guthrie offered Merrithew some advice on how to get the men the recognition they sought. "When the York picture comes out and is being shown, it will then be current news and it will serve to refresh the memory of the different people in Washington who, unquestionably, in my mind, did not go into this matter and give credit to all who participated."[48] This idea, of course, would only work if the roles of the men were properly depicted in the film.

As for Warner Bros.' failure to pay the men, Merrithew and Kornacki continued to discuss methods to get all the men a fair sum. On March 27, 1941, Kornacki wrote to Merrithew to say he would do his best to get some of the local American Legion members and other veterans to write to Washington about York's true personality. Kornacki also mentioned that he still had not received any money.[49] Merrithew and Kornacki pushed to get the American Legion and Veterans of Foreign Wars involved, which resulted in some success.

On April 10, 1941, Roy Obringer wrote to Jesse Lasky about the complaints of the men. He said that since the press covered the story about the release payments, "every other week I receive a complaint either from the Veterans of Foreign Wars or the individual survivors." Obringer cited Merrithew's March 11 letter where he said he wanted the picture to give credit or recognition to what actually took place and warned that they must be careful not to libel any survivors.[50] Obringer brought this point up again in another communication on April 16, where he listed the names of the survivors who were giving them the most trouble: Otis Merrithew (principal "beefer"), Percy Beardsley, Joseph Kornacki, Mario Muzzi, Michael Sacina, George Wills, Feodor Sok, Thomas Johnson, and Patrick Donohue. Obringer suggested that if none of them was represented in the movie, then "they can be forgotten." Obringer warned, however, that on the one hand, if they did not use their names, they could claim an invasion of privacy by portraying their characters incorrectly. On the other hand, if they did use the names, then it would possibly give credence to their claims to be paid $250.[51] Thus, the studio needed to find a way to placate the men to avoid any future legal trouble.

Patrick Donohue turned to Flanigan & Fox of Lawrence, Massachusetts, for legal help to get his money, and the firm contacted Warner Bros.' New York office on his behalf. In response, Obringer wrote to the New York office with instructions. His letter revealed tensions within Warner Bros. about the surviving members of the patrol. He revealed that Lt. Col. Edward Danforth had "demanded and received $1500" for his signature, which pushed Guthrie to get the signatures of the other men at the best price possible. Once Merrithew got $250, Guthrie again pushed to secure the other releases for the best bargain he could. Obringer said that many of the survivors got $50 while Donohue received $5. He continued, saying "unfortunate publicity got out at the time whereby Guthrie was credited with having paid each of these survivors $250. Storms of protests have been received by us since. The Veterans of Foreign Wars headquarters

EXECUTIVE OFFICES
321 WEST 44TH STREET
NEW YORK

TELEPHONE
EXCHANGE
HOLLY 1251

PICTURES, INC.
WEST COAST STUDIOS
BURBANK, CALIFORNIA

March 18, 1941

Mr. Otis B. Merrithew
17 Whitney Street
Chestnut Hill, Mass.

My dear Otis:

     I just returned to the office this morning and found your airmail letter of February 24. You know we are making two pictures with the Navy and I have been at sea where I could not get in touch with my office; hence, the delay in answering your letter. I will only be in here for a day or two and am again leaving for another three or four weeks at sea.

     Now, as to York being down here—he positively has not been here since last September and he will not be here at all. I perfectly agree with you when you say that Mr. Lasky is making a mistake by not having you here to help with the battle sequences of the picture. However, I have done everything that I can to have them send for you but it is beginning to look very doubtful.

     About the advice you asked for—I'll tell you what I think, Otis, and I believe if you think it over you will agree with me. When the York picture comes out and is being shown, it will then be current news and it will serve to refresh the memory of the different people in Washington who, unquestionably, in my mind, did not go into this matter and give credit to all who participated. I am certainly most heartily in accord with anything that you want to do to open up the matter. This however, is between you and me.

     As to any more money that might be sent to the rest of the boys, I have turned this over to our Legal department and recommended that it be paid. However, you know how those things are and how slow they are at times.

     As soon as I come back to the office I will probably have more to tell you about the ultimate plans for the picture. Anyway, please bear in mind that I sincerely believe you have both feet on the ground, and anything you want to do will have my sanction, but remember this is only coming from an employee and not from a member of Warner Bros. Picture Corporation; in other words; I am just a little boy trying to get along.

Mr. Otis B. Merrithew - 2   March 18, 1941

Otis, I appreciate your letters very much, and especially the good wishes from your good wife and the children. I brought some more match cases back with me and I am sending them on to Anne. You will notice some of them are from Honolulu and from the U.S.S. Richmond. I am going to try to get cases from as many of the battle-ships as possible.

With kindest regards and very best wishes to all, I am

Sincerely yours,

W. L. GUTHRIE

Letter from William Guthrie to Otis Merrithew, March 18, 1941. Courtesy of Jimmy Fallon.

in Kansas City, Missouri is conducting an investigation, and I have correspondence on my desk requesting an explanation, which I might say, will be rather difficult and embarrassing to answer."[52]

Obringer continued to discuss the ramifications of this problem within the studio. Legally, the studio had the releases and could make the film undisturbed. However, he revealed that he was aware there were allegations of "misrepresentation and fraudulent inducement" for the signatures. Obringer suggested to Jack Warner and Jesse Lasky that they increase the release payments to $250. This would, he hoped, "stop the flood of protests, the investigation by the V. F. W. headquarters, and eliminate possible unfavorable publicity and boycotting of the picture." As for the question of fraudulent inducement, Obringer said it was "difficult to pin Guthrie down to what actually took place in his securing of the various releases."[53]

Obringer's letter also reveals that he had spoken to Jack Warner several times about "paying these people off and getting rid of them," but he wanted to rely on their legal standing with the releases.[54] Obringer understood the bad publicity that could arise from ignoring the men and their claims. Fortunately, the argument finally gained enough attention that the studio was forced to act.

On May 9, 1941, Guthrie preemptively wrote a letter to Merrithew to inform him that Jack Warner had finally instructed the studio's legal department to see that each of the survivors be forwarded enough money to bring the total to $250 each. He asked Merrithew for suggestions about how to deliver the money to the men.[55] The next day, Obringer sent an official announcement to Warner Bros.' New York branch. Raising each man's payment to $250 would cost the studio $1,835, but it was justified considering the potential negative criticism and the further possibility of a whispering boycott campaign among veterans.[56]

In order to avoid any more bad press and keep costs down, the studio decided to let the Veterans of Foreign Wars (VFW) national headquarters track the men down. Obringer noted that headquarters had already requested detailed information and an explanation of how and from whom these releases had been secured, as well as the amount of consideration paid. If the studio delegated the job of securing survivors' signatures on the new documents to the VFW, then it would stop any further protest or complaints and also gain the support of the organization. By paying the men, the studio hoped it would be free of "any further claims, annoyances, or threatened boycott" from the survivors.[57]

The survivors finally began to receive their payments in May 1941. On May 21, Kornacki wrote a letter to Otis Merrithew informing him that he had finally received his money. He told Merrithew, "I can't quite make out how you went about getting the money, but you have done it and is the main thing."[58] Despite this small victory, Merrithew was still not happy about not being allowed to know how the picture would handle the battle scene. He wrote another letter to Jesse Lasky on June 29, 1941. He bluntly told Lasky: "the $250 doesn't by any means give me any satisfaction unless I can be assured that I am to have a prominent part in the picture's battle scenes." Merrithew warned Lasky that if the movie did not show the correct story, then he would put the other survivors' perspectives together in a book. Merrithew would also reveal how "yellow York really is" and how throughout the war York kept repeating that he wanted to go home. Merrithew also argued that York had treated the survivors poorly in the past and that the picture had better not betray the truth.[59] Unfortunately, in addition to worrying about the studio's ability to show the truth, the media once again capitalized on the payments of the men to further misrepresent them in the press.

From June 30, 1941, through July, an article by John Chapman and another one by Paul Harrison, circulated around the country. These articles followed the pattern set by the Frederick C. Othman January 10, 1941, article that had described the survivors' situations when Guthrie found them. However, the second round of articles in the summer of 1941 added new details and changed some locations.

This time Percy Beardsley was in Roxbury, Connecticut, cutting wood on his farm when his father met Guthrie and demanded to know why he visited. Once told, the father declared "Perc, I kinda like this feller. Fetch out the pitcher," and they drank hard cider and toasted to the old days.[60] Beardsley and his father raised oxen.[61]

In Boston, Otis Merrithew, a city truck driver, lived with his wife and three daughters. Guthrie did not ask why he had enlisted under the name Cutting.[62] In any case, he accepted Guthrie's $250 so that his eldest daughter could attend at least one year of college. "I wasn't going to be able to send her to college next year, but now I can."[63] In Lawrence, Massachusetts, Guthrie found Patrick Donohue. There were no recalled details.[64] Chapman's version claimed that Guthrie bought him a suit of clothes.[65]

In Holyoke, Massachusetts, Guthrie found Joseph Kornacki with his six children. Kornacki, who was pleased at the prospect of being portrayed in a movie, was a mill worker. Bernard Early worked as a waiter in a cheap restaurant in Hamden, Connecticut[66] In a dingy tenement in Manhattan's "Italian Quarter," Mario Muzzi worked as a night watchman. It took Guthrie three hours to convince Muzzi to take the money.[67] Chapman claimed that Muzzi's mother said "there's something funny here. You get no money for nothing any time," which caused the long discussion.[68]

Also in Little Italy, Michael Sacina worked as a porter in a barber shop. Guthrie then found George Wills in Philadelphia at the edge of the city dump living in a lean-to shack. Wills was an unkempt man whose companions were four long-haired goats. Feodor Sok lived in Buffalo at a veterans' Civilian Conservation Corps camp.[69] One paper, the *Albany Times-Union*, commented on the camp where Sok worked: "we know these camps were established to get veterans like Feodor into the backwoods and away from the public eye."[70]

Finally, Guthrie located Thomas Johnson in Denison, Texas, living in a one-room house. When Guthrie entered, he found dishcloths, suspended from a line in the center of the room to make a partition. They carried out their conversation without looking at each other. The release and money were passed over the line.[71] In Harrison's version, Guthrie says that he only saw Johnson's eyes. "Maybe he was naturally shy. Possibly he was a war-ravaged monstrosity. Guthrie, remembering those burning eyes and the talk they had, doesn't like to guess."[72] These sad stories created a depressing image of the men for the American public just as the film premiered. The press coverage revealed just how poorly Warner Bros. represented the story and misrepresented their actual lives.

This fight to receive payment for their releases reveals the issues involved in dealing with Warner Bros. When Merrithew wrote his first letter to Jesse Lasky on June 12, 1940, he did not seek payment. His only concern was getting proper recognition for him and the other men in the portrayal of the battle. Warner Bros. offered the money with the idea of "paying these people off and getting rid of them," as Roy Obringer said.[73] Seeing that a fight with the studio could not be won, the men signed the releases either because of their financial situations or because they believed that they would finally receive credit for their roles in the October 8, 1918, engagement. However, the studio took advantage of their situations to pay them very little. With these signed releases, Warner Bros. was able to reduce the men's role to a minimum. The media also used the meagre payments as a way to show how poor and unnoteworthy their lives were in comparison to Alvin York's. By presenting the public with these false images of the other men, the media aided York and Warner Bros. by insinuating these were men who would say or do anything to get a larger piece of the fame and fortune that came with the movie. This further diminished any claims they brought to the public.

On July 1, 1941, Alvin York gave a radio address on the *We the People* radio show. In this address, he made the following comment: "Although I was credited with practically wiping out the whole battalion of 35 machine guns, I was only one of the 17 who did the job. Anyone of the other boys could have done the same thing I did if fate had put them in my place. If any of my buddies are listening in tonight, I want them and the whole world to know that without their cool courage none of us would be alive today."[74] Despite this attempt to mend the rift between the men on the eve of the movie's premiere, the damage had already been done. The timing of York's radio address suggested his only interest was in calming the tensions that had arisen around the movie.

On July 2, 1941, the movie *Sergeant York* premiered in New York City at Broadway's Astor Theater. The Warner Bros. publicity department went all out for the opening. They orchestrated a VFW parade down Fifth Avenue, with hordes of veterans marching to the theater. Alvin York and Jesse Lasky arrived in a convertible limousine and joined other

VIP guests such as General of the Armies John J. Pershing, former Commander-in-Chief, AEF, New York City Mayor Fiorello LaGuardia, Gary Cooper, and others.[75] The Astor Theater was adorned with a four-story likeness of Cooper as York made of 15,000 flashing lights that changed the image from a "hillbilly carrying a squirrel gun to a soldier carrying a rifle." The US Army also used the movie for recruiting by handing out eight-page pamphlets to young men along with hard-selling recruitment material.[76] The White House even held a special screening for President Franklin D. Roosevelt, who then invited York to visit on July 30, 1941.[77]

The screenwriters attempted to balance godliness and patriotism in their representation of true Americanism in the movie. To do this, the writers took dramatic license, often further exaggerating the York legend beyond even the Cowan and Skeyhill books. This expanded the myth beyond the military world, which gave it a wide audience and cemented it in the minds of many Americans. The film's writers invented a scene where York proved his marksmanship on the firing range in order to show York being interviewed by his company officers. The interview scene between Maj. G. Edward Buxton and York was also created to temper the perception of York as a religious fanatic.[78] These changes may seem insignificant, but they are now firmly part of the public conception of the York myth, despite being the creations of Warner Bros. writers. The scenes reinforced York's religious convictions and provided proof that he embodied the characteristics needed to become a righteous Christian warrior in France.

The beginning of the movie shows York at a turkey shoot in the Tennessee hills, setting up the infamous scene where he picks off a line of Germans by shooting the last soldier first, then moving forward down their line while they charged at him. This detail of the story has persisted ever since 1919 when George Pattullo wrote his article in the *Saturday Evening Post*, although Pattullo said nothing about firing from back to front. Pattullo's original article only said that a unit charged York and that he shot them all because "at that distance, I couldn't miss."[79] Samuel Cowan added the back-to-front method in his 1922 book, *Sergeant York and His People*.[80] Never mind that in an interview with the *New York Herald Tribune* after the premiere of the movie, York admitted that the technique for shooting turkeys "did not apply to his capture of 132 Germans."[81]

Of the "Other Sixteen," only Bernard Early had much of a role in the movie. The others are casually named and only once. Early is erroneously portrayed as a drill instructor and sergeant, who hazes York for his religious beliefs during training. Once in France, the sixteen do not have any time on the screen until the battle begins. It was the fear of this poorly researched battle scene that sparked Merrithew's crusade to get proper recognition for the other survivors from Warner Bros. Guthrie had told Merrithew that the scene might refresh the memories of military officials in Washington, who would then realize they had not given appropriate credit to all who participated in the battle. Unfortunately, this important scene, the center of the story, could not have been further from the truth.

Script writers Howard Hawks and John Huston improvised wildly to alter the battlefield scenes. They played up the myth that York had destroyed thirty-five machine guns, when in fact, York claimed he had only taken out one.[82] The writers knew about the other survivors' accounts, yet did not use them at all in the script, as evidenced by Abem Finkle's statement quoted earlier. In addition, Harry Parsons, who had not been an eyewitness to the engagement, gave a ridiculous statement about the battle and how he had fought alongside York, which was used for the movie. He said that "York got into a trench and moved around and came upon the troops, and I came face to face with a sniper. My rifle was clogged from sand, and when I fired the barrel opened up and burst. I lay on the ground and fired a pistol at this sniper until I got him."[83]

The battle scene reflects Parsons's false description as well as popular American perceptions of the war. The movie shows the Argonne Forest with long lines of trenches, destroyed trees, and shell craters defacing the landscape. The men charge across a barren field, dodging barbed wire and diving into shell holes for cover. In reality, the action took place in a dense forest in a sector that had few trenches because it had not been on the frontline during the war. In the movie, the men follow Bernard Early into a trench, where they engage a German unit before continuing up the hill. The patrol then uses this trench to get behind the machine gun nests, completely disregarding Early's skillful leadership in moving his men, unseen, through the forest.

After the machine gun fired upon the group wounding Early and Merrithew, the movie shows Early yelling to York: "You're the only non-com left. Takeover, York." This scene confirmed the myth that York took charge of the patrol during the engagement. The most accurate part of the battle scene shows other men firing at the Germans along with York. However, when the officers and York return for the Medal of Honor investigation, they say that the other men had not been firing, which meant York must have killed all the Germans.

It is understood that Hollywood takes liberties with movies to enhance the stories it wants to tell. Nevertheless, *Sergeant York* became so influential that it permanently skewed the legend into a mythological tale of Alvin York. The other survivors—if they were lucky—had their name mentioned within the film. Warner Bros. had their sworn statements from Merrithew and read their complaints. The studio had the opportunity to include their perspectives but left them out in order to appease York. The myth Warner Bros. created continues to the present day, perpetuated by historians who cite the same stories the movie used as a reference, namely, Skeyhill.

After seeing the film, the other survivors attempted to bring their story, which Warner Bros. had spurned, to the public. In a letter of July 14, 1941, Merrithew told Early: "it is time for us to do something about Sergt. York. As you know, we are getting the wrong end of the stick . . . we all realize we will never get what belongs to us unless we go after it."[84] The same day, Merrithew drafted the story of the other survivors and sent it to the *Boston Globe*. This letter was never published in the newspaper, but a copy was sent to Warner Bros. and another saved by Merrithew. (See appendix 2.)

In short, Merrithew claimed that none of the survivors agreed with the portrayal of the battle in the movie. The men claimed that they had not signed the affidavits intentionally, and that if they had signed them, it was during a period when they were constantly signing documents given to them by their supply sergeant. Bernard Early, Otis Merrithew, Percy Beardsley, Patrick Donohue, Joseph Kornacki, and Feodor Sok signed or agreed to have their names added to the letter. The fact that the *Boston Globe* never published Merrithew's document and that a copy was sent to Warner Bros. suggests that the media did not want to speak out against the film.[85]

Bill Guthrie shared the disappointment in the film's portrayal of the battle. In a letter to Merrithew of July 25, 1941, he said:

> I too have done a lot of cussing, especially Lasky and some of the people at the Studio who made the suggestion that I take the matter up with you concerning the technical work on our picture. I want you to know, Otis, that this hurts me like the dickens. By all means you are the man who should have done the technical work on this picture.

> I advocated all the way through and, in fact, was told to write
> you long before I did. I did not want to build up your hopes in any
> way, but please understand, Otis, this is not a censor in anyway, and I
> am not blaming you, but had you not written your first letter to Lasky
> concerning the survivors etc., you would have been a cinch. They gave
> the argument that they were afraid you might cause a little trouble.
>
> I want you to understand that I do not blame you for writing the
> letter and protecting your buddies, and I know that had you thought
> a second time you would not have done so.[86]

This letter shows that Merrithew's zeal to defend the story of the other survivors cost him the chance to guide the story on film. Warner Bros. knew that the story was not as York and Skeyhill had originally told it, but still chose to move forward with their own version.

The studio's lack of attention to the other men also revealed itself in Jesse Lasky's autobiography, published in 1957. Despite producing the movie and being part of the conversations regarding the portrayal and credit of the other men, he was either completely ignorant of their stories or lied to discredit these men. He writes: "The search afforded an illuminating study on the fates of war heroes. One was in jail; another was wanted by police and had to be approached by an ad in the paper and a secret rendezvous. One family was destitute, with seven children, and in their case a bigger check was written than the usual $100 gratuity."[87] Jesse Lasky's claims are in complete contrast with the true lives of the men. He became another public figure to attack the reputations and character of the men, thus adding to the public misconception of the survivors.

The release of the movie also drew senators to the theater, and they brought discussion of the battle into the Senate. Senator Kenneth D. McKellar of Tennessee wished to introduce a bill to the Senate to award Alvin C. York the rank of colonel and place him on the retired list. This bill had been passed by the Senate before but failed in the House of Representatives. Senator McKellar assured the Senate "that the bill has not grown out of the new fame which has come to Sergeant York by reason of the excellent picture." He argued that York's distinguished service deserved to be rewarded. Senator John A. Danaher of Connecticut asked Senator McKellar if he knew of the role played by Early or the others in the engagement that he believed York should be rewarded for. In response, McKellar stated:

I do not remember the name of the particular person. Sergeant York was aided by those who were with him. If the Senator will examine the history, he will find that Sergeant York became separated from his companions, and himself did the work which his companions afterward approved. They were in the same organization. I do not recall the particular name mentioned by the Senator, but if the Senator says that a particular man was with Sergeant York, or in the same organization with him, I have no doubt that his statement is correct. I do not dispute it at all. However, Sergeant York was by himself when he killed 25 Germans and captured the other 132.[88]

Senator Danaher responded to this on August 7, 1941, by reading to the Senate the recommendation that Maj. Edward C. B. Danforth wrote in 1929 for Early's DSC. He hoped to "supplement the efforts of Representative James A. Shanley to the end that Corporal Early be given proper and just recognition for his participation in this now famous exploit."[89] Despite their optimism, Bernard Early received no further recognition for his role in the engagement as the popularity of Warner Bros.' version captivated the American public.

This failure to rectify Early's role in the official record did reveal a long-standing problem with the US War Department. During the discussions, Senator Alexander Wiley of Wisconsin brought up the stubbornness about fixing records. Of the War Department, he said, "the danger to the country is that when we have a department which will not recognize that it has made a mistake and will not try to rectify it."[90] Clearly, the senators understood that the War Department would not admit to its faults, even at the expense of the truth.

The success of Sergeant York dealt a final blow to the attempts of the other sixteen men to gain recognition. The mythologized film version of Alvin C. York and his role at Chatel-Chéhéry on that October morning pushed the other men out of the historical narrative finally and completely. Being exploited for their releases, being misrepresented in the media, and not being recognized in the film left these men virtually forgotten. They were marginalized in the story of Alvin York. Although the movie effectively pushed these men out of the spotlight, they, especially Otis Merrithew, continued to push to have the true story of their involvement known through the next two decades.

7

Few Acknowledge It

On August 1, 1941, theaters withdrew the movie *Sergeant York,* and Warner Bros. postponed its general release until July 4, 1942. Senators Gerald P. Nye of North Dakota and Bennet Champ Clark of Missouri introduced Senate Resolution 152 that called for a thorough investigation of the film industry by the Committee on Interstate Commerce. The senators felt that with the film Hollywood had violated America's official neutrality and tried to turn public opinion toward favoring the war. When the committee singled out *Sergeant York,* Warner Bros. pulled it out of its limited release until the committee completed the investigation.[1]

During the hearings, Harry Warner took the stand in defense of the movie. He described *Sergeant York* as "a factual portrayal of the life of one of the great heroes of the last war. If that is propaganda, we plead guilty. . . . These pictures were carefully prepared on the basis of factual happenings and they were not twisted to serve any ulterior purpose."[2] The committee continued its investigation until the United States declared war on Japan on December 8, 1941.[3]

Just as the limited release had upset the other survivors, the general release of the film in 1942 upset other veterans. Pvt. Arthur Ward, who also served in Company G, 328th Regiment, 82nd Division, expressed his feelings in an article for the *Sunday Herald* of Bridgeport, Connecticut. He bluntly called Alvin York a coward who inflated his role. Ward said the credit belonged to Otis B. Merrithew. Ward said he had not spoken up sooner because he was not the only war veteran "wise to York but the hoax spread like wildfire so talking would do no good because Washington will not take back a medal." For over twenty years, Alvin York sat by and allowed the story to swell until the movie brought a climax too nauseating for Arthur Ward. He believed the movie "itself was a fraud and 'blew up' York."[4]

Ward revealed that when the surviving members of the patrol had rejoined the 1st platoon of Company G., Acting Cpl. York told his company commander, Capt. Edward C. B. Danforth Jr., all about his own heroism, leaving out the other men from the raiding party. Ward also said that York may not have left all of his hell-raising in the past. Instead, he was a bad sport around camp who incited fights with other men.[5] Ward would not be the only one who felt that the movie had done an injustice to the other men. The "single-handed" part of the story and its portrayal in the movie became the main point of contention with many others.

The government received numerous letters from disgruntled citizens upset over the movie's single-handed portrayal. A Mrs. George S. Barnes wrote to the US War Department asking for clarification. "Why do they *now* feature Alvin York, our World War Hero No.1 as having captured—'single handed'—the 132, Germans, when the records in Washington read—'fearlessly *leading seven men*, he charged a machine gun nest'—etc. (With *seven more* to help him). . . . I would like very much to know the names of the *other seven* men who have been given no publicity at all."[6] Some citizens felt that the story was unjust to the survivors and other veterans because it singled out one man.

After the release of the movie, most of the other survivors abandoned their efforts for recognition. World War II captured the country's full attention. Some of the men participated in the war effort. Merrithew, for example, worked at the Boston Navy Yard. Only Patrick Donohue carried the fight for recognition during the war. In February 1945, he officially received his Silver Star Medal from the War Department as a result of efforts initiated by the Lawrence Veterans' Affairs Department and Congressman Thomas J. Lane.[7]

After the war, Merrithew again renewed the fight for proper recognition. He wrote to representatives, senators, and presidents hoping that someone would help him receive recognition. He finally made headway when his daughter, Jeanne Merrithew Faye, wrote to Senator Edward M. Kennedy of Massachusetts on February 4, 1963. She told the senator that her father had not been officially decorated by the Department of the Army for his part during the engagement on the morning of October 8, 1918, and that he "is getting along in years now, and this injustice is uppermost in his mind." She mentioned that Senator David I. Walsh of

Massachusetts had opened a case with the Department of the Army, but nothing had come of it. She closed by asking Kennedy to investigate the matter.[8]

Senator Kennedy responded to this inquiry by opening an investigation to ascertain what could be done for Otis Merrithew.[9] The senator relayed the request through his office, which checked the Military Affairs records, but those only went back to 1938. They transferred the request to the Library of Congress to find the original congressional documents. Kennedy's inquiry revealed that the bill had been presented to the House of Representatives by Robert Luce on December 11, 1929, but did not make it out of the House Committee on Military Affairs.[10] In response, Jeanne Faye asked the senator to reopen the case and find out why the bill did not make it out of the Committee in 1929.[11] Unfortunately, the senator did not proceed with any legislation on Merrithew's behalf.

On September 2, 1964, Sgt. York died at the age of 76, and on September 9, Merrithew penned a letter to Senator Kennedy. Now that York had died and his story was again in newspapers around the country, Merrithew felt it was an opportune time to seek the long overdue recognition and credit. He believed that Senator Walsh had recommended him for the Medal of Honor in 1929 and asked that it be awarded because of the "grave injustice done to me when history was made." Merrithew also said he had been writing a book on his life in order to tell the truth about the other survivors. However, if he would be awarded it, he could let the argument rest.[12]

Senator Kennedy at this time opened a formal inquiry with the Department of the Army. Army Adj. Gen., Brig. Gen. L. H. Walker Jr., in response to Senator Kennedy's inquiry, revealed that Merrithew had not been recommended for the Medal of Honor. Instead, Merrithew had been recommended for the DSC in 1932. As it had earlier, the US Army fell back on the old excuse of the cutoff date of May 26, 1928, stating that the recommendation "was not received within the time limits prescribed by law and, therefore could not receive favorable consideration."[13] Kennedy's assistant sent the letter from the adjutant general to Otis Merrithew with regrets.

Undeterred, Merrithew responded by asking the senator to present another bill to Congress to award him the long overdue DSC. He attached a copy of the sworn statements from 1929, which several of the other men signed. Merrithew argued: "I think that you will have to agree that I got a raw deal. I happen to be the only one that was not decorated. I think due to the fact that I was in the service under another name and that the other 5 buddies were trying to locate me for years."[14] Merrithew did not receive a response from the senator.

On February 8, 1965, Merrithew sent another letter to Kennedy asking for assistance in receiving the DSC for which he had been recommended. This letter too went unanswered.[15] Finally, on June 18, 1965, Merrithew tried once more to obtain assistance from the senator. Obviously frustrated with the system, Merrithew said that "every senator after Sen. David I. Walsh up to you has pigeonholed that recommendation to give me that medal. Don't you think it would be the proper thing before I pass on to take it out of that hole that it has been in all these years and cheer up my last years on Earth?"[16] This plea, too, did not receive a reply.

On August 12, 1965, Merrithew wrote a personal letter directly to the president of the United Sates, Lyndon B. Johnson, asking for his assistance in receiving the DSC. He wrote in part: "I was recommended for the Distinguished Service Cross. Since that time, I have had Senators David Walsh to Sen. Edward Kennedy tell me that they could not do anything for me. Now I [am] asking you what can be done for me. My doctor has given me a few more months to live and I would be very pleased to get that medal before then."[17] This final plea brought a positive response for the first time in 47 years. On September 8, 1965, Merrithew received an official response from Lt. Gen. J. K. Woolnough: "The President," he said, "has asked that I reply to your recent letter concerning your eligibility to receive the Distinguished Service Cross. Your letter is receiving attention and further reply will be made within the next few days."[18]

On September 13, 1965, Merrithew officially received news that he would finally receive the long overdue formal recognition for his role during the engagement so many years before in the Argonne Forest. Lt. Gen. Woolnough wrote: "I have the honor to inform you that, by direction of the President, you are entitled to the award of the Silver Star for gallantry in action in France in World War I."[19] Newspapers across the country printed the announcement. They noted that the Army did not explain the long delay in awarding Merrithew.[20]

Before the official ceremony to award him with the Silver Star, which was scheduled for October 21, 1965, at Fort Devens, Massachusetts, Merrithew began to receive congratulations from groups that had supported his earliest attempts at being recognized. The Eighty-Second Division

Otis B. Merrithew is awarded the
Silver Star for WWI Heroism at
Ft. Devens Open Officer's Mess by
Maj. Gen. Charles S. O'Malley Jr.,
October 22, 1965.
US Army Photograph.

Association expressed happiness about "finally getting the belated medal
due you so many years ago." The division also formed a small committee to be present at the official ceremony.[21] The Board of Selectmen of
Brookline, Massachusetts, which had originally pushed Merrithew to
seek recognition in 1929, congratulated him for having "at long last,
received the well-deserved recognition."[22]

On Thursday, October 21, 1965, 47 years after the engagement at Chatel-Chéhéry, the US Army held a formal awards presentation ceremony
to award Otis B. Merrithew the Silver Star Medal. At Fort Devens, Massachusetts, Maj. Gen. Charles S. O'Malley Jr., commanding general, XIII
Corps and Fort Devens, Massachusetts, pinned the Silver Star medal onto
Merrithew's proud chest. Representatives of the 82nd Division Association, Stephen F. Rutledge Veterans of Foreign Wars Post 864, more than
100 friends and family, and XIII Corps and Post staff officers attended
the small ceremony. Merrithew's citation reads as follows:

The President of the United States of America, authorized by Act of Congress, July 9, 1918, has awarded the Silver Star to Otis B. Merrithew (then private), 1910252, Company G, 328th Infantry. On October 8, 1918, in the action West of Chatel-Chéhéry this soldier, when his company was held up by enemy flanking fire, with several other crawled to the flank and killed or captured the enemy who were delivering the flanking fire.[23]

After the presentation of the Silver Star, Merrithew addressed the crowd. He expressed his appreciation for the honor rendered to him by his country. He then commented on the current affairs surrounding protests of the Vietnam War, saying "those who burn their draft cards—those objectors—that minority who do not honor their country. If our forefathers had acted as they are acting—if our forefathers had this attitude, where would our country be today?" Ever patriotic, he concluded his speech by leading them in song to "Don't Bite the Hand That's Feeding You."[24]

Once he returned home, Merrithew wrote a personal letter to President Lyndon B. Johnson on November 4, 1965. Merrithew thanked him

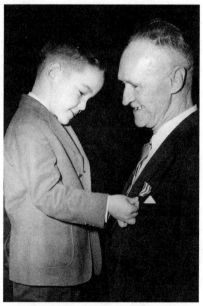

Jmmy Fallon admires Silver Star awarded to his grandfather Mr. Otis B. Merrithew for WWl Heroism. October 22, 1965. US Army Photograph.

for his help and sent along a photo of his grandson, Jimmy Fallon, and himself after being awarded the Silver Star at the award ceremony and expressed his sincere appreciation to the president for finally making it possible to receive an award for his role in the fighting on October 8, 1918. His entire family signed the letter as a token of their thanks.[25] President Johnson returned the photo and his best wishes.

Merrithew was not through, however. In December 1965, he wrote a letter to Lt. Gen. J. K. Woolnough to determine why he had received the Silver Star instead of the DSC for which he had been originally recommended in 1932. Army Adj, Gen. Maj. Gen. J. C. Lambert replied on December 7, 1965, that the US Army awarded the Silver Star on the "basis of an official determination that there was sufficient evidence of record to conclude that your name should have been included in orders issued in 1919 citing certain members of your organization for gallantry in action. This determination made you eligible for the Silver Star which was recently awarded you." This suggests that the Department of the Army reviewed the letter from Col. Julian R. Lindsey in 1930. Curiously, it conflicts with the War Department's denial of the Silver Star recommendation in 1933 when they claimed they had no record of any citation for Merrithew. The letter from Lambert also restated that Merrithew had been recommended for the DSC in 1932, but the law that was put in place had prevented him from receiving it.[26]

Over the years, Merrithew had lost touch with most of the other survivors, many of whom had died in the early 1960s. In fact, Merrithew believed that he had become the last living survivor of the October 8, 1918, engagement. To his surprise, however, Percy Beardsley sent him a letter on January 3, 1966, in which he congratulated Merrithew on receiving the Silver Star but revealed that "I never did . . . guess I won't make effort to get it. If it could be done quietly, perhaps, but it might require a lot of red tape and excitement which I am now physically unable to go through." Beardsley never received his official award but took comfort in the fact that Merrithew finally got his due. He concluded his letter by stating: "My wife and I have no children . . . so you at least have a family to leave a Silver Star to!"[27]

After finally receiving recognition, Merrithew continued to remember that fateful battle and the men killed. Every year he would raise his flag above his house to commemorate the battle. He would still talk to reporters and tell them about how Alvin York "stole all the glory" and how the other men should have all received the attention and praise due to them.[28] Unfortunately, most of the other men died without receiving any official recognition or award. Their lives after the war are as follows:

HEADQUARTERS
DEPARTMENT OF THE ARMY
OFFICE OF THE ADJUTANT GENERAL
WASHINGTON, D.C. 20315

IN REPLY REFER TO

AGAC-SC-P Merrithew, Otis B.
1 910 252 (6 Nov 65)

7 DEC 1965

Mr. Otis B. Merrithew
17 Whitney Street
Chestnut Hill, Massachusetts 02167

Dear Mr. Merrithew:

This is in reference to your recent letter to General Woolnough, concerning your entitlement to the Distinguished Service Cross rather than the Silver Star which was recently awarded to you.

The Silver Star was awarded to you on the basis of an official determination that there was sufficient evidence of record to conclude that your name should have been included in orders issued in 1919 citing certain members of your organization for gallantry in action. This determination made you eligible for the Silver Star which was recently awarded you.

Our records show that you were previously informed that to be considered for the award of the Distinguished Service Cross for World War I service, you must have been formally recommended for the award within the time limits fixed by law. The law governing the award of decorations for World War I service permits consideration only of those recommendations which were received in the War Department before 26 May 1928. A recommendation in your behalf for award of the Distinguished Service Cross was received in 1932. However, this recommendation was not received within the time limit fixed by law and therefore, cannot be considered.

Sincerely yours,

J. C. LAMBERT
Major General, USA
The Adjutant General

Inclosure

Letter from Major General J.C. Lambert to Otis Merrithew, December 7, 1965. Courtesy of Jimmy Fallon.

Joseph Kornacki received an honorable discharge from the US Army on May 27, 1919, and returned to his home in Holyoke, Massachusetts. On August 23, 1920, he married Rose Dolat. They had eight children. He was an active member of Post 25 of the American Legion. He continued working at the American Writing Company. On March 27, 1959, Joseph suffered a heart attack and died on the way to Holyoke Hospital. He is buried at Mater Dolorosa Cemetery, South Hadley, Massachusetts.

Feodor Sok became a naturalized citizen on November 20, 1919. It appears that he moved to Ashley, Pennsylvania, sometime in the 1920s and married a woman named Stefia Hock in 1928.[29] The 1930 census, however, lists him as single and working as a coal miner; there is no mention of his wife.[30] He later moved to Buffalo, New York, and became a member of the Veterans' Buckhorn Civilian Conservation Corps Camp on Grand Island.[31] He died on January 27, 1960, and is buried at St. Matthews Cemetery, West Seneca, New York.

Bernard Early spent six months in a French hospital after the battle with little improvement. Eventually, a French doctor determined that there still might be more shrapnel in him. They opened him up again, found it, and removed it. He spent several months in France recovering before being able to return home. Once home, he worked as a bartender and restaurant owner. He married Catherine Hines and had four sons and a daughter. He died on April 11, 1961, and is buried at Saint Lawrence Cemetery, West Haven, Connecticut.

Thomas Johnson returned to Lynchburg, Virginia, and worked as a stock clerk in the Beasley Shoe Company. In the 1920s, he and his brother John moved to Denison, Texas. He lived a quiet, secluded life, nursing nerves shattered by his experience in World War I. He spent most of his later years in and out of veterans' hospitals. He died of a heart attack on September 23, 1961. He was interred at Fairview Cemetery, Denison, in a simple graveside rite "with the obscurity that eclipsed his fame as a fighting buddy of Sgt. Alvin York."[32]

Patrick J. Donohue returned to Lawrence, Massachusetts, and worked as a mill worker. He did not speak much of the war or his role in the famous engagement. He died on February 8, 1962. He is interred at Bellevue Cemetery, Lawrence. Upon his death, Representative Thomas J. Lane of Massachusetts told his story in Congress to "insert in the Congressional Record the story of Paddy Donohue's courage."[33] After his funeral, his Purple Heart and Silver Star were supposed to be sent to his sister in Ireland. However, it seems that the Silver Star, at least, never made it. In 2016, a retail assistant at ReStore, a thrift shop in Andover, Massachusetts, found the inscribed Silver Star in the drawer of a dresser that had been dropped off by an anonymous donor. After turning the medal over to the Andover Town Clerk, city employees tracked down Patricia Waters, Patrick's great niece, and presented the medal to her.[34]

George Wills married Elizabeth Doris Buck in 1920. They had three sons during their marriage. He died on April 20, 1962, in Philadelphia. He is buried at Sunset Memorial Park, Feasterville, Pennsylvania.

Michael Sacina lived in Manhattan after the war. He owned and operated the tobacco concession in the International Magazine Barber shop located in the Hearst Building on West 57th Street. He married Elizabeth Addieg and had two children. He died on April 23, 1966, and is buried at Long Island National Cemetery, East Farmingdale, New York.

Percy Beardsley returned to his father's farm near Roxbury, Connecticut. His father, Nathan Beardsley, ran a champion Devonshire cattle farm which was considered the leading breeder in the eastern United States. Percy continued working the farm after his father's death. He married Louise Lingsch. Beardsley died on September 17, 1968. He is buried at Roxbury Center Cemetery, Roxbury, Connecticut.

Otis B. Merrithew held several jobs after the war. He became a chauffeur with the Brookline Highway Department and then volunteered as a crane operator at the Boston Navy Yard during World War II and the Korean War. He continued as a crane operator at the Watertown Arsenal and finally worked as a security guard at the Faulkner Hospital in Boston. Always a hero, on July 3, 1930, Merrithew stopped a runaway car by chasing it down and jumping into it before it reached a lane of traffic.[35] He married Mary O'Hara, and they had three daughters. Otis was an avid coin collector; he was also a poet and loved to have sing-alongs around the piano with his family during holiday events. Every October 8th and November 11th he would sing one of his favorite songs—"Over There."[36] He died on April 21, 1977. He is buried at Walnut Hills Cemetery, Brookline, Massachusetts. After his death, the city of Brookline held a ceremony on October 8, 1977, dedicating the intersection of Whitney Street and Meadowbrook Road as Corporal Otis B. Merrithew Square.[37]

Mario Muzzi returned to the United States after the war and married a woman named Concetta. He continued working as a baker for the National Biscuit Company (later Nabisco) at the bakery on West 15th

Street, New York City. He became a US citizen on January 12, 1923. Muzzi retired to the town of Civita di Bagnoregio, Italy, dying there in April 1978, at the age of 90.

Muzzi's death finally marked the end of the "Other Sixteen" and their long-fought battle to receive formal recognition for their roles during the engagement on that October morning at Chatel-Chéhéry so many years prior. After sixty years, only a few of the men received any sort of official credit or recognition. Out of the ten surviving members of the patrol, excluding York, only three, Cpl. Bernard Early, Pvt. Patrick J. Donohue, and Pvt. Otis B. Merrithew, received any official decoration for valor from either the War Department or the Department of the Army for their role during the engagement on the morning of October 8, 1918.

In the case of Otis Merrithew, he never received the DSC for which he had been rightfully recommended. Various governmental agencies were or have been approached for assistance in securing these decorations, but they continually cited the statute of limitations that prevented Merrithew from being formally awarded the DSC. However, this time limit has finally been lifted. On February 10, 1996, the National Defense Authorization Act was officially passed by Congress and officially approved and signed by the 42nd president of the United States, William J. Clinton, which finally repealed the statute of limitations that had been set in place on awarding official US military decorations and valor awards to American service members for past military conflicts (including World War I, World War II, and the Korean conflict).[38]

The story of the "Other Sixteen" shows how the War Department, the US Army, Hollywood, and the public pushed aside the men, including Alvin York, in order to transform the story into an American epic myth. Despite being part of the official record in official brigade orders, War Department citations, and presidential orders, the other men have been forgotten in the story of the battle of Chatel-Chéhéry. As *The Evening Sun* reported in 1965, "In 1918 the United States needed a hero. Destiny tapped a gangling soldier from Tennessee, Alvin York, once a conscientious objector. He became a hero, but he had help. Most heroes need help. But few acknowledge it."[39] Indeed, few acknowledge the role the other men played in that battle.

York's original story included the other men. But when Maj. Gen. George Duncan used the story to enhance his own reputation, he exaggerated it by suggesting the other men did not play significant roles.

Subsequently, George Pattullo, Samuel Cowan, and Thomas Skeyhill further altered the story and added parts to what became the legend, namely, that York's feat was a single-handed one and they also added the "turkey shoot." Hollywood then piled on other details to the story and cemented the myth through its popular film. However, the other men still hoped their story would be given weight. It seemed that their deaths would squarely remove them from the story of Alvin York. And in some ways, this was correct. After their deaths, historians continued to use Alvin York's story to enhance their work, but they further twisted the original story by including information on the other men of the patrol during and after the battle.

8

Perpetuation

After the deaths of the patrol's survivors, their stories were finally inserted into the Alvin York narrative. However, the addition of the other men into the tale followed a negative trend as historians continued to reiterate the "single-handed" story even as they looked into the survivors' attempts to gain recognition after the war. Unfortunately, instead of researching into the claims of the other survivors, authors simply wrote them off as jealous and greedy men driven by the desire to acquire the same wealth and fame that York had received. Thus, the distorted stories of the other survivors became a new addition to the myth. It was not until 2018 that their roles finally received closer consideration. After 100 years, the perspectives of the other survivors seemed to be given equal weight. And yet, authors still skewed their stories to fit them into the Alvin York myth.

In 1963, twenty-two years after the release of the movie, and with only four of the original members of the patrol still alive, Laurence Stallings, a Marine Corps combat veteran of World War I, published *The Doughboys: The Story of the AEF, 1917–1918*. In his retelling of the October 8, 1918, battle, Stallings gave Bernard Early more credit for his role in the engagement and described the lead up to the firefight when Early fearlessly led the men through enemy lines and decided to attack despite being outnumbered. Stallings then recounted that the other men scattered for cover while York did the fighting alone. Despite the overall description of a single-handed fight, Stallings's book marks the first time another member of the group received even minimal credit in the story.[1]

Perhaps one of the most damaging additions to the historiography of the other survivors' stories comes from Robert Ellis Cahill, a folklorist and author who wrote books about New England covering many diverse topics ranging from ghosts and pirates to scuba diving and military history. On May 24, 1970, Cahill published an article about Otis Merrithew in the *Sunday Herald Traveler* (later republished in his book *New England's Little Known War Wonders* in 1984). Cahill had met Merrithew and went through his collection of documents related to his push for recognition. Unfortunately, however, Cahill did not work with Merrithew when he was writing the article. Despite meeting Merrithew and viewing the documents he possessed, Cahill's work is full of false information and incorrect details. Cahill's biggest flaws are the "quotations" he suggests came directly from Merrithew. Many of these quotations are in stark contrast to Merrithew's opinions and documentation. Cahill's final "quotation" is the speech Merrithew gave after receiving the Silver Star in which Cahill claimed Merrithew acknowledged that Alvin York deserved all the credit for acting single-handedly.[2] Later historians would use this citation as validation that York was indeed the true hero of that battle. However, the official press release from the Information Office of Fort Devens, Massachusetts, where the ceremony was held, does not mention anything about Alvin York. In reality, Merrithew closed his speech by leading those in attendance in singing "Don't Bite the Hand That's Feeding You."[3]

Fortunately, in 1985, David D. Lee looked at the story of Alvin York with a more careful eye. His research into Thomas Skeyhill's research revealed the underlying issues and myth-making parts of his work. Lee's book, *Sergeant York: An American Hero*, attempted to cut away the legend and myth surrounding York's upbringing and religious convictions. Lee attempted to look at the real Alvin York instead of following Cowan and Skeyhill's path in creating a legendary figure. Unfortunately, however, Lee, too, perpetuated the single-handed myth. He mentioned that Bernard Early led the men, but once Lee got to describing the battle, he discussed only York's role in fighting the Germans. Lee is the first author to talk about the other survivors during the filming of the movie *Sergeant York*, briefly noting that Bill Guthrie, the Warner Bros. agent, tracked down the men and paid them $250 for their releases. Lee also cited Jesse Lasky's autobiography, which falsely claimed that one of the men was wanted by the police and had to be contacted through a newspaper advertisement. The sources used by Lee and subsequent historians created an atmosphere of doubt about the other survivors' stories.[4] This served as the newest addition to the myth of Sgt. Alvin York, that the other survivors were jealous of York's success and that they had lied about their roles in the battle.

In 1997, John Perry, an infantry veteran and editor for *Home and Christian Life Review*, wrote *Sgt. York: His Life, Legend and Legacy*, in which he aimed to tell the full story of Alvin York from his upbringing to his death, with all of York's troubles included. Yet, when it came to the "Other Sixteen," Perry insinuated that their questioning of York's story showed that the other members of the group were "tired, bored, jealous, or had a change of heart." Perry is the first to cover some of the attempts the other survivors made to receive credit in the 1920s and 1930s. While he discussed the Connecticut American Legion's support for awarding Early the Medal of Honor, Perry used the incident to accuse Early of being jealous of York's fame. Perry also discussed Merrithew's attempts to recognize the other men in the film *Sergeant York*. However, Perry portrayed Merrithew as a troublemaker who saw "there was some big Hollywood money to be made, Merrithew thought he deserved some of it." Perry portrayed the other survivors as untrustworthy and greedy and gave no credence to their claims. He even went so far as to claim that all the survivors wanted "a little more recognition and cash."[5]

Fortunately, Michael E. Birdwell, who worked as the curator of the Alvin York Papers, brought a new perspective to the story of Alvin York in his 1999 work *Celluloid Soldiers: Warner Bros.'s Campaign against Nazism*. A wonderful look at Hollywood's work to counter Nazi ideology, his book contains two chapters on the movie *Sergeant York*, which included Otis Merrithew's effort to get an accurate portrayal of the other men's role in the battle. Unfortunately, the work leans heavily toward York's perspective, stating that the other men "proved frustratingly uncooperative." Birdwell also includes incorrect information about the other men's awards, such as claiming that Merrithew received a DSC in 1927, making them look greedy for money rather than wanting their roles portrayed correctly.[6] This is likely due to the lack of accessibility of documents from the other survivors, but it reflects the available sources on the topic at the time.

The transition into the 21st century brought new opportunities and made additional sources available to those who sought to use the myth of Alvin York. Commemorations, new research, and anniversaries defined the next twenty-one years. However, those who discovered new evidence would face an uphill battle to counter the myth as others strengthened the story even more and brought it back to mainstream thinking.

In 2000, the Sgt. York Patriotic Foundation, which had been founded in 1993, began publishing a quarterly newsletter for visitors to the Sgt. Alvin C. York State Historic Park entitled *Sgt. York Says*. In addition to reporting on current events about the Foundation, it also contains parts of York's story and letters. These publications have been distributed to thousands of visitors who read them as official stories. Unfortunately, the Sgt. York Foundation relies on Tom Skeyhill's version, and therefore their official message is that "practically unassisted he [York] engaged and whipped a German machine gun battalion, killing 28 of the enemy, capturing 35 machine guns, and bringing in 132 prisoners." The other men "took little or no part in the actual fighting."[7] The Foundation presents the story as if the other men were not involved at all and therefore deserve little to no credit.

As the 100th anniversary of America's entry into World War I approached, more historians began to look into the larger context of the country's participation in the fighting. In 2008, Edward G. Lengel, a well-known historian and relative of York, published *To Conquer Hell: The Meuse-Argonne, 1918, The Epic Battle That Ended the First World War*. Lengel's work is one of the best books on the Meuse-Argonne Offensive, but at the same time it is an example of works that cover the battle and tend to follow the accepted story of Alvin York. This does not reflect on Lengel's historical method but shows the incestuous nature of the resources readily available on York. When discussing the 2nd Battalion, 328th Regiment, 164th Brigade in the battle, Lengel focuses on York and even calls the brigade "Corporal Alvin C. York's outfit." He gives Early credit for leading the men, but he also writes the story in a way that shows York taking a larger role in the decision making. Lengel gives York all the credit for the fighting. He claims the other men "emerged cautiously from behind trees and underbrush and helped guard the prisoners." Lengel then says that York gave orders and led the men out of the woods.[8] The surviving men are portrayed as cowards who hid during the fighting while York did most of the work.

The early 2000s also saw the publication of new work on locating the site of the battle. Between 2000 and 2006, Col. Douglass V. Mastriano, USA Ret., worked to find the original engagement site. In 2006 he excavated what he believed to be the correct location. Despite finding various

American and German artifacts, scrutiny of his research reveals that he was not at the correct location.[9] Mastriano has nevertheless persisted in his view and published the most recent biography of Alvin York in 2014, *Alvin York: A New Biography of the Hero of the Argonne*. Mastriano's approach harkens back to that of George Pattullo, focusing on York's religious conviction as a large part of the story. In his introduction, Mastriano calls attention to the way York's detractors belittle his beliefs, which Mastriano sees as a reflection of the postmodern negative view of faith. In his eyes, an attack on York's faith as the basis of his accomplishments merely reflects contemporary cynicism. Mastriano also discusses historians who question the accuracy of York's feat and claims that his own research and evidence show that York played the largest role in the action, with some assistance from Percy Beardsley. However, Mastriano says that Beardsley "took the honorable road" and did not discuss his actual role. Despite this slight acknowledgment and conceding that the other men provided some covering fire, Mastriano says they played "a role, albeit a lesser one, in the action." Mastriano gives York overwhelming credit for the fighting and taking charge.[10]

Mastriano upholds earlier versions of the story and increases the mythical aspects even though he had access to a wealth of new primary research. In 2008, Bernard Early's grandnephew, Robert D'Angelo, gathered together many descendants and relatives of the other sixteen men from the patrol. Together, they gathered original documents, letters, articles, and more that revealed a new side of the story. In a sense, they had the half that was missing or had been dismissed by those who contributed to the myth of Alvin York.

This group of relatives reached out to Mastriano and offered their assistance to have their relatives brought back into the story. Instead of adding their stories to the record, Mastriano chose to attack the characters of the other men. "When a disgruntled veteran comes forth," Mastriano says, "he finds a willing press interested in controversy, all in an effort to sell papers." Mastriano also claims that the press gave the other men "a prominent platform to attack York. Indeed, jealousy is a powerful emotion, and it would turn men who once fought shoulder to shoulder against each other."[11]

Instead of considering their roles in the battle, Mastriano accuses the other members of being motivated solely by jealousy. Mastriano also claims that Merrithew started a "campaign in the early 1920s against the U.S. Army to secure an award for himself." There is no evidence of this intent. Mastriano repeats claims of jealousy and greed when discussing the *Sergeant York* film and the men's attempt to get recognition. Mastriano often refers to Robert Cahill's book to show that Merrithew supported York, even though Cahill fabricated much of the information. Mastriano's work led to numerous opportunities to write articles and lectures as well as a trail and monument at the site in France where Mastriano claims the battle took place. Mastriano's book, and the attention it generated, perpetuated and even elevated the mythical version of the story.

The American Battle Monuments Commission would also use the York myth. In July 2018, it released the *World War I Battlefield Companion*, which promoted Douglas Mastriano's "Sgt. York Trail." The guidebook's short description of the engagement mentions only York and "seven privates." It also provides an incorrect timeline, giving readers a misleading summary of the battle. This official guide relegates the other men to an unnamed, miniscule part as "a number of Americans" or "seven privates."[12]

In 2017, Laura A. Macaluso published *New Haven in World War I*, which tells the story of New Haven, Connecticut, and its contributions and stories of World War I. Macaluso's work is conspicuous for its omission of one of the town's most significant World War I connections: Bernard Early. She does not include him or discuss his role in the war. Macaluso does not even mention the fact that the city celebrated "Bernard Early Day" on October 12, 1929. with a massive parade and celebration. While she may have had her reasons for the omission, Macaluso's choice to exclude Early is a perfect example of how the other survivors faded into obscurity, even in their own hometowns.[13]

Fortunately, another group was also working at the battle site in France during the same years as Mastriano (2006–2009). Dr. Thomas J. Nolan had formed a team with the goal of combining geographic information science (GIS) with archaeology as a way to help interpret battlefields. This work became Nolan's dissertation in 2006, and the team undertook a second expedition in 2009 to perform a more complete excavation of the site. Most of Nolan's findings were not published until 2018, when team member Michael Kelly published *Hero on the Western Front: Discovering Alvin York's WWI Battlefield*. Kelly's book focused on the debate with Col. Douglass Mastriano over the location of the October 8, 1918, battle. The present work, *The Other Sixteen*, agrees with Michael Kelly and Dr. Tom Nolan's conclusion that they discovered the correct site of where the October 8 engagement took place. Their conclusion is based on archaeological evidence and primary research that Mastriano does not provide.

Kelly released the findings of Dr. Nolan's research in order to counter the mythical version of the battle that so many authors have promoted. Nolan and Kelly met the descendants of the sixteen and viewed their primary material. This finally brought attention to their story, especially because Kelly mentions their histories in an appendix entitled "The Other Sixteen." Kelly's appendix contains much of the information from the former website that the descendants created, *www.theothersixteen. org*. However, Kelly only lists fifteen of the sixteen; he excluded William Wine and replaced him with Harry Parsons. Kelly also introduces the first criticism of the Medal of Honor investigation, listing the men's affidavits and discussing their inconsistencies.[14]

Even with the new documentation from the other men of the patrol, the 100th anniversary of the battle in 2018 brought out new publications that continued the old tropes and myth of Alvin York. That year, the US Army Center of Military History published commemorative brochures of the US Army Campaigns of World War I, including the *Meuse Argonne: 26 September–11 November 1918*. While this brochure does say that Bernard Early led a reinforced squad that surprised and captured several Germans, it still gives York all the credit after he told the men to take cover. The brochure also credits York with killing fifteen to twenty-five Germans and capturing or destroying thirty-five machine guns. This short and inaccurate description of the battle shows the Center of Military History's deep misconceptions and ignorance about October 8, 1918.[15]

In October 2018, the Association of the United States Army (AUSA) released a graphic novel called *Medal of Honor: Alvin York*. They chose this format to expand the reach of AUSA's educational mission to a younger audience. Unfortunately, the AUSA repeated the same single-handed myth. The novel does not mention the name of any of the other sixteen. The artwork shows York, rather than Bernard Early, initially leading the patrol. It also portrays York fighting the Germans alone with no assistance from anyone else. This novel's final inaccuracy is the statement that the Germans surrendered to eight Americans, when there were still eleven men, counting York, alive after the battle. The AUSA may indeed have a mission to "honor those who have served in order to advance the security of the nation." But they completely left out sixteen soldiers.[16]

Finally, in 2021, James Carl Nelson published *The York Patrol: The Real Story of Alvin York and the Unsung Heroes Who Made Him World War I's Most Famous Soldier*. While Nelson's book has the veneer of including the stories of the other survivors and their roles in York's story, he combines many different versions of the myth and adds to them. The book's opening finally corrects some issues associated with the story, such as ranks and who was originally in charge. However, when Nelson reaches the battle, he retells the same old narrative, now rife with incorrect details, such as the German machine guns on top of Hill 223 swinging "their weapons around, saw events unfolding below, and after shouting to their comrades to hit the dirt let loose."[17] Nelson also frequently criticizes the perspectives of the other survivors and their attempts to receive recognition.

Nelson acknowledges that during the battle, Percy Beardsley returned fire with his Chauchat and pistol. However, the other survivors' roles in the firefight are dismissed with York's account of "two men sniped at the Boche."[18] Nelson claims that Otis Merrithew and Mario Muzzi both "froze in the bush with their wounds."[19] Echoing past authors, Nelson portrays Sgt. York once again "almost by his lonesome" in the battle; the lone hero complete with the mythical turkey shoot.[20] Nelson also glosses over the survivors' return to the American lines and insinuates that Bernard Early and Otis Merrithew were both incapacitated upon their return and thus they could not have been in charge of the patrol.

After the events of October 8, 1918, Nelson appears to concentrate on convincing readers that they should not trust anything the other survivors say. Nelson's book is supposed to present the "full" story, which brings in the perspectives of the other survivors. However, he consistently belittles their opinions or casts doubt and shame upon their claims. He portrays Bernard Early as a nagging, jealous man who just coveted the attention and fame that went to York. Nelson says that upon his return "Bernard Early was . . . grumbling to "friends" . . . that he and the other ten survivors from the patrol . . . had not received their due."[21] Otis Merrithew is a constant target of Nelson's attacks. Nelson describes Merrithew's claims as "bogus" and implies that Merrithew only wanted attention, money, and a "shiny star."[22]

The York Patrol also mishandles the historic timeline. Nelson constantly moves events around his narrative such as the payments of the survivors from Warner Bros. For instance, he presents the story of Otis Merrithew receiving his payment as the last one to do so. This makes Merrithew appear greedy since he received "two hundred more dollars than his peers."[23] However, Merrithew was the first to receive the payment, and he assumed the other men would receive the same amount. Nelson's mishandling skews the story, ensuring that some individuals will appear greedy, conniving, or otherwise filled with ill will. He also states that the other survivors were filled with "bitterness and jealousy" when they sought recognition, thereby showing that the prejudice against the sixteen is still alive today.[24]

After the deaths of the other sixteen men who fought with Alvin York on October 8, 1918, the myth of Alvin York continued. Historians attempted to add new details, but no solid primary sources from the other survivors were made available until 2008. Even when they did have access to these documents, authors continued to rely on tired tropes instead of seeking to tell the original story of Alvin York; a story of seventeen men.

9

October 8, 1918

To reconstruct what happened to the entire patrol on October 8, 1918, the account presented in this chapter relies on the following consensus: If at least three sources in the various accounts of the American survivors, interviews, and affidavits agreed on an event, it was included. While we will never be able to confirm exactly what happened in that ravine, combining the perspectives offers new insight into the battle. This consensus-based approach, together with recently verified archaeological evidence and original German documents, will create a story that reflects the perspectives of all the survivors.

Early on the morning of Tuesday, October 8, 1918, the men of the 328th Regiment began to push through the Argonne Forest near the French village of Chatel-Chéhéry, France. From their jump-off positions, they began their attack at approximately 06:00 while advancing into a thick ground fog. They were to advance with the 327th Regiment on the right flank, the 328th Regiment in the center, and the 110th Regiment, from the 55th Brigade, 28th Division, AEF, on the left flank, all advancing west toward their objective. Unfortunately for the Americans, the preceding artillery barrage and the expected advance of the 110th Regiment never materialized.[1] Nonetheless, the Americans continued to advance with little resistance for about 700 meters, until suppressing enemy machine gun fire from the front and both flanks enveloped the 328th Regiment.

2nd Lt. Kirby Stewart was leading his platoon from the front when a burst of enemy machine gun fire hit his leg and knocked him down. Even though he was wounded, the determined lieutenant continued to lead his men forward. He was encouraging his men to continue the attack when

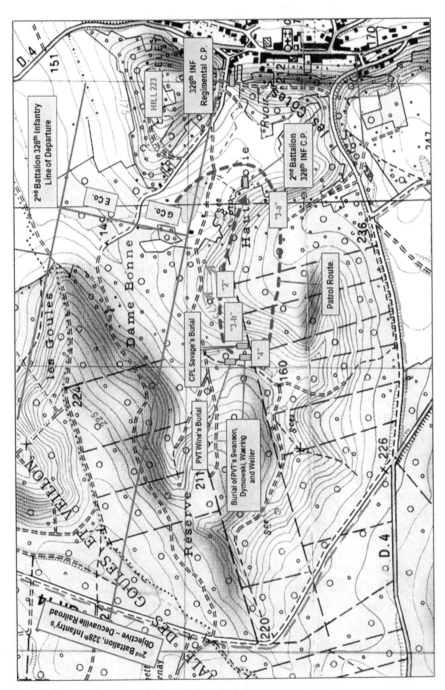

Map of the patrol's route and location of the firefight. Courtesy of Brad Posey.

| Patrol Route |
| LTC Buxton's letter to CPT Swindler |

"The advance of the battalion was stopped not only
by heavy fire from the front which was expected, but
chiefly by continuous bursts of machine gun fire from
the nose southwest from Hill 223 about where I have
written the figure "2".

"Early led a skillful reconnaissance in which the 3 squads
crawled back under the cover of the brush on Hill 223 and
circled southwest on the route shown as "3-a" gaining the
crest of the hill due-west from the hostile fire. Early could
hear voices from the west and straight down the wooded hill
in the direction of "4".

The machine-gunners picked up on the return route, about
due east to the valley (shown as "3-b") must have been
survivors of the fight on the hillside and those still further to
the west who had been flanking the battalion and whose
position is shown as "2".

another bullet struck him in the head killing him instantly.[2] Command then fell to Plt. Sgt. Harry Parsons. After surveying the situation, Sgt. Parsons ordered Cpl. (Acting Sgt.) Bernard Early, to lead three squads—seventeen men in all—around to the left rear flank of the enemy, where they could take out the machine gun positions that were holding up their unit.[3]

By around 08:00, the seventeen-man patrol was advancing through the valley and woods to reach its objective behind the German lines. Acting Sgt. Bernard Early led the patrol of three squads, which were in turn led by Cpl. Murray Savage, Pvt. (Acting Cpl.) Otis Merrithew, and Pfc. (Acting Cpl.) Alvin C. York. York's squad was armed with a Chauchat automatic rifle.[4]

After advancing about 150 meters, without losing a single man, the seventeen-man patrol reached the base of the hill where they jumped into a boundary ditch and followed it up and over the hill to reach the other side. They carefully pushed through the forest with the drum of heavy machine gun fire coming from the ridge above them. The men continued until halting in the underbrush at a small stream where they listened for movement. Sensing the presence of someone, one of the men shouted out requesting identification. After a few tense moments, a German soldier darted from his hiding place. Shortly after, another German soldier rushed out. The Americans fired their weapons but missed when the first

German tripped, allowing both to escape into the cover of the woods. The pursued Germans swung to the right.[5] Acting Sgt. Early split his small force into smaller combat groups and continued the advance.

They slowly pushed forward until Cpl. Murray Savage called out "There are the Boche!"[6] Early's group was the first to stumble upon a group of Germans who appeared to be sitting down to a meal. The enemy soldiers, who belonged to the 1st Battalion, Landwehr Infantry Regiment 120, along with 15 to 20 newly arrived men from Reserve Infantry Regiment 210, had laid down their weapons to eat breakfast.[7] They were neither in a hurry to do anything nor concerned about being on alert.[8] The seventeen Americans converged around the unsuspecting Germans and opened fire. Fifteen to eighteen Germans immediately fell.[9] The surprised enemy threw up their hands in surrender. while others set out on the run. Seeing what was happening, Early declared "this is murder, cease firing."[10] This surprise firefight caused the Germans to surrender to the small group of men, whom they believed were part of a larger American force. Among the first men captured in the initial group were Lt. Paul Vollmer, often described by Americans as a German Major, and Lt. Karl Glass who had been inspecting their company's defensive positions; they were closest to York and his squad. They were sent over to join the rest of the prisoners.

Acting Sgt. Early then ordered York and the men with him to keep the Germans covered while the others disarmed them. The Americans lined the Germans into two rows. Although the numbers vary, the consensus of several men is that around 80 to 90 Germans surrendered to the patrol. Early then searched the front row while Merrithew searched the second. One of the officers surrendered his pistol to Merrithew while they were lining up the Germans. Early then walked over to Pvt. Joseph Kornacki to tell him to keep close to the Germans on the march back to the American lines.[11]

Before he could finish his sentence, however, a platoon of Sappers from the Bavarian 7th Mineur Company that were on the slope above the Americans, who were dealing with the prisoners, noticed the commotion below and signaled the captured Germans to lie down.[12] The prisoners immediately dropped to the ground, and the Bavarians opened fire on the unsuspecting American squad with a single machine gun and rifle fire.[13]

Acting Sgt. Early went down immediately, hit in the arm and side with at least four wounds. Although severely wounded, he remained conscious and passed command to Acting Cpl. Merrithew.[14] Six of the other Americans were killed in the fight. Cpl. Savage was shot through the stomach and died while attempting to crawl to shelter.[15] Pvt. Dymowski was shot twice and died instantly.[16] Pvt. Swanson was shot through the neck causing almost instant death.[17] Privates Wareing and Weiler were both killed almost instantly.[18] Private Wine managed to fire a few shots from his rifle before being killed.[19]

Pvt. Muzzi was wounded through his shoulder and crawled to safety. Merrithew began returning fire with the other men around him but soon received a wound in the left arm. Determined, he continued to fight from where he knelt using his revolver with his right hand.[20] During the engagement, Merrithew never lost consciousness, nor did he relinquish command of the surviving members of the patrol.[21] Pvt. Beardsley took cover behind an oak tree and returned fire with his Chauchat automatic rifle, accounting for several dead Germans.[22] York took cover in a clump of bushes beside a tree. Private Kornacki crawled into cover around the captured Germans and returned fire on the enemy. Privates Sok, Wills, Donohue, and Sacina moved in close around the German prisoners, realizing how outnumbered they would be if the prisoners were to stand up.[23] Sacina singled out Lt. Vollmer and kept his rifle on him throughout the fight.[24] The Americans knew that the only way to avoid direct fire from the slope was to stay close to their German prisoners. The battle raged in the ravine for approximately ten to fifteen minutes.[25]

During this intense firefight, Acting Corporal York, who had been the closest to the Germans on the slope, moved into a better firing position. From his vantage point, he managed to kill several Germans on the slope while they focused their fire on the other men. Pvt. Beardsley, who was near York, fired his Chauchat automatic rifle until he either ran out of ammunition or it jammed. Both of his ammunition bearers had been killed.[26] Beardsley then pulled out his service pistol and continued firing at the Germans. Together, Beardsley and York killed or wounded several more Germans on the slope.

While the Americans were able to dive behind trees and into holes when fire erupted from the slope, the German prisoners were exposed to the fire from their own men. It tore into them, wounding and killing several of them.[27] At some point during the battle, several Germans rushed toward the sound of the firefight. York saw this and fired at them hitting the first man in the abdomen; then he killed or wounded a

couple of others before they could scatter for cover.[28] Becoming aware
of the carnage and chaos, Lt. Vollmer blew a whistle and called for the
Germans still fighting to cease fire and surrender.[29] The Germans on the
slope obeyed their officer and surrendered to the Americans.

Even though he had been wounded, Pvt. Merrithew was still standing
and in charge of the patrol. He had three bullet holes in his helmet, his
gas mask was shot off, and a can of corned beef in his back pocket had
been smashed by bullets. He had suffered a few wounds to the left arm but
only one severe enough to require a simple operation. As Lt. Col. Edward
Buxton later put it, these were "all flesh wounds."[30] Merrithew ordered
his men to line up the prisoners into a column of twos and march them
back to the American lines. Beardsley wrapped his overcoat around the
wounded Early, and then he and Donohue began to carry their leader
back toward the rear. They quickly ordered several German prisoners to
carry him so that they could guard the column.[31]

To reach their lines, the Americans and their prisoners had to march
through the German frontline. The Americans compelled Lt. Vollmer to
march at the head of the line and threatened him with his life if he did not
get the defenders to surrender. Merrithew ordered York to march at the
front.[32] York kept his pistol at the small of Vollmer's back. On their way to
the American lines, the men encountered more German soldiers, whom
Lt. Vollmer commanded to surrender. This included Lt. Max Thoma and
his orderly who had been rushing toward the gunfire they had heard to
the right rear of their position. After about 100 meters, they encountered
the Americans and their prisoners. Lt. Thoma had no choice but to also
surrender.[33] On the way back to the American lines, the men and their
prisoners were struck by a German artillery barrage, which forced them
to rush back to safety. During the barrage, a piece of shrapnel caught Pvt.
Patrick Donohue in the left shoulder.[34]

When the American patrol emerged from the woods and reached
its own lines, they met other members of Company G, including 1st Lt.
Joseph A. Woods, battalion adjutant, 2nd Battalion, 328th Regiment,
and Plt. Sgt. Harry Parsons. At this point, York led from the head of the
column while the other men walked along each side of the prisoners.
Pvt. Merrithew walked along the left flank of the column "yelling like a
mad man."[35]

Acting Sgt. Early was taken from the German prisoners who were carrying him and placed on a stretcher. He had a hole in his back so large his

Clinical Record Brief of Otis Merrithew,
Evacuation Hospital 28, October 16, 1918.
Courtesy of Jimmy Fallon.

kidney was visible.[36] Upon seeing the wounded American soldiers arrive, Sgt. Parsons took Merrithew to the temporary 2nd Battalion aid station to have his wounds dressed. Merrithew showed Parsons the German pistol he had acquired from the German officer and stated, "I got what I went for."[37] When Merrithew exited the aid station, he found that 1st Lt. Woods had placed Acting Cpl. York, the only nonwounded noncommissioned officer, albeit an acting one, in command of the prisoners and ordered him to take them back to the regimental headquarters. Woods had also counted up their prisoners and recorded 132 in all.[38]

However, before York headed back toward the regimental rear area with the German prisoners in tow, 1st Lt. Woods gave him five more men from another platoon of Company G to act as additional guards as well as several more prisoners who had been captured by other units. Merrithew and Early were both present when Woods gave his instructions to York,

Graves of Fred Wareing, Maryan Dymowski, Carl Swanson, and Ralph Weiler.
Signal Corps Photograph.

and they accompanied the surviving members of the patrol until they reached ambulance row. At this point, Merrithew, Early, Donohue, and Muzzi were loaded into field ambulances and taken back to the rear for further medical attention.[39]

York then took the surviving members of the patrol along with the German prisoners back to the 82nd Divisional prisoner pen. When Acting Cpl. York arrived in the divisional rear area with the prisoners, he was reportedly asked by Brig. Gen. Julian R. Lindsey, "Well, York, I hear you have captured the whole damned German Army," York stated, "I only [have] 132."[40]

The battle that took place on October 8, 1918, would color the rest of the survivors' lives. But one man, Alvin York, found himself thrown into the center of the story. Despite his wishes and the wishes of the other survivors, outside groups altered and exaggerated the story into a legend until Warner Bros. created a new myth with *Sergeant York*. An experience shared by seventeen became a "single-handed" encounter, with Alvin York as the sole hero. York could not extricate himself from the myth,

Grave of Murray Savage. Signal Corps Photograph.

nor could the other survivors effectively correct the record. Commanding officers, the US Army, the War Department, and Hollywood promoted the myth for their own advantage, with the survivors attempting to get their due credit along the way. After their deaths, their stories faded away until their descendants gathered together and worked to preserve their memory. The work of the survivors and their descendants paved the way for this book to finally record the story of the "Other Sixteen" lost in the myth of Sgt. Alvin York.

Epilogue

By Robert V. D'Angelo Jr.

I want to thank James Gregory for writing *Unraveling the Myth of Sgt. Alvin York*. His book makes a compelling case that the battle near Chat-el-Chéhéry on October 8, 1918, was not a one-man show by Alvin York and that the other patrol members played a much more significant role in that iconic battle than was previously recognized or acknowledged. Through exhaustive research, James uncovered extraordinarily important material never before considered. He also used crucial information gathered by our descendants' group to preserve the memories of our relatives and develop a more nuanced and accurate understanding of what happened that day.

The story of that battle has fascinated me for close to sixty years. Why? Sgt. Bernard J. Early, the leader of the patrol, was my maternal grandfather James's youngest brother and a beloved uncle to my mother. At 97, my mother still has his wedding photo on her living room wall and vividly remembers the parade and dinner honoring Sgt. Early, which followed his receiving the Distinguished Service Cross in 1929. At the award ceremony in Washington, Secretary of War Hurley reportedly said to Sgt. Early that DSC could well stand for "Damn Slow Coming."

Growing up in New Haven, Connecticut, with the Earlys, I often heard about Sgt. Early's role in that famous engagement in France. Sgt. Early was a local hero, especially to Irish Americans of which there were many in New Haven. He had immigrated along with his two brothers and sister from Mohill in County Leitrim, Ireland. Most Irish Americans in New Haven at that time were from Leitrim, which was one of the poorest counties in a poor country, and so Sgt. Early's prominent role in the battle and his recovery from the serious injuries he sustained were a source of family and community pride.

In addition, from time to time, usually close to the anniversary of the battle or on the death of one of the participants, an article would be published in the local New Haven newspaper. I still have the very yellowed original article I clipped out from the November 8, 1964, *New Haven Register* entitled "New Haven's Forgotten Hero—Should Bernard Early Share Alvin York's World War 1 Honors?" The article, by Frederic Kelly, was written not long after Alvin York's death. It begins as follows:

> To the end he refused to talk about it. 'I'm no hero,' he'd say and his blue eyes would snap in anger. Yet there were those who refused to believe him, those who considered New Haven- bred Sgt. Bernard J. Early . . . every inch a soldier, but too damned modest.

The article ends on a similar note about his reticence:

> Early's widow, who lives in Hamden and is suffering with a heart condition, believes there is more to the story. 'My husband', she said, 'didn't get the credit he deserved. I'm sure of it. But how will we ever know . . . he never would talk about it; he just never talked about it.

But others did talk about it. And what was said was exactly that: he and the other members of that patrol never received full or proper credit for the events of that day. So why did Sgt. Early insist he was no hero? Was it false modesty? I have concluded from my research over the past few years and time spent with other descendants that what he meant was that he was no more of a hero than any of the other men in that patrol, including Alvin York. In other words, neither he nor any of the others would have sought honor and recognition were it not for the wildly disproportionate honors bestowed on Alvin York and the hagiographic story of his "single-handed" capture of 132 Germans. Implicit in that version is that the others did little or nothing, and that was wrong as many knew and as James Gregory demonstrates.

In 2005, with Internet sources available, I embarked on a search to learn more about what happened. Almost immediately, I discovered that the York matter continued to generate heated controversy almost 90 years after the battle. Two groups of historians—one led by Professor Thomas Nolan and Michael Kelly, and the other by Douglas Mastriano—were attempting through battlefield archaeology to pinpoint the precise location of the famous engagement with Alvin York. Their work was attracting international attention, due in part to articles published by Craig Smith of *The New York Times* and other prominent commentators. It seemed clear, however, that for both groups my great uncle and the members of the patrol other than York were, as they always had been, at most supporting players whose roles were to confirm the York legend.

My curiosity piqued, I did more research. I read most, if not all, of the standard works on the subject starting with George Pattullo's original *Saturday Evening Post* article from 1919, through Samuel Cowan and Skeyhill, and up to the more recent books.

A few things struck me about this material. First, they often contained factual errors, even, almost unbelievably, about basic details such as the names and fate of the patrol members other than York. Second, they mostly all accepted without question the original accounts, including those of Pattullo, Cowan, and Skeyhill. And third, other than for the formulaic and highly suspect affidavits of some of the patrol members (the originals of which James Gregory incredibly discovered, thanks to the help of Steven Girard, and which he discusses at length in this book), they are not based on the accounts of those patrol members who were actual eye witnesses but by others who were not and who seemed anxious to bask in reflected glory.

What to do about this? Was there anything to the Sgt. Early account of a group effort? I decided to take a different approach to find out. First, I searched for previously unknown accounts by the surviving patrol members. Some of those might be in sources such as local newspapers or privately published histories. And second, I looked for descendants of the surviving patrol members who might have heard stories similar to those I had from family through the years or might even have letters or diaries describing the battle. I set out on a mission to find those sources and descendants for each of the surviving patrol members (other than Early and York, of course).

The newspaper sources were not often easy to find but they were there. In fact, in 1920, less than two years after the battle, Sgt. Early gave a detailed description of the battle in an article in the Connecticut newspaper, *The Hartford Courant*, which, as James Gregory details, differs dramatically from the York version. And, very importantly, Percy Beardsley was interviewed at length about the battle by a reporter for his hometown Connecticut newspaper, the *Waterbury Republican*, in 1927. The reporter notes that "it is hard to get Mechanic Beardsley to talk about this experience."[1] Percy was the embodiment of all of the New England types rolled into one: the taciturn farmer, country bumpkin (who really isn't) and rustic wit. Beardsley was a Connecticut Yankee, the descendant of five generations of Connecticut Yankees. His great-great- grandfather was a soldier in the American Revolution and was crippled from the wounds he received in that war. His ancestors, who like him were farmers, lived in picturesque Roxbury, Connecticut, which has evolved from a farming town to a weekend retreat for affluent New Yorkers.

The reporter was himself a World War I veteran, which, he posited, might have caused the usually taciturn Percy to open up a bit about his role in the battle. The reporter noted that even Percy's father, Nate, was unable to draw the story out of him. Nate told the reporter that he would pit Percy's marksmanship against York's any day since Percy was known as a crack shot in his hometown of Roxbury. Crucial to the facts of the battle, Percy describes in the article using his Chauchat automatic rifle and .45 sidearm to effect during the battle, information that did not appear in the record previously. Interestingly, forensic evidence of those unique 8 mm Chauchat casings and the .45 casings that were located by the archaeological teams on the battlefield support Percy's account in the estimation of those teams. Other than in James's book, I have never seen any reference to this *Waterbury Republican* article, which, incidentally, also contains one of the best analyses of why York was honored to the exclusion of the others and notes near the end that "[t]he organizations of ex-service men have always been more or less skeptical of York's exploit."[2]

Many more local newspaper accounts of the battle were published in which the survivors described their experiences, particularly in 1929 at the time of the War College event. Other than myself and James, I do not believe most commentators even looked for these accounts, much less reviewed or considered them.

The search for descendants of the survivors ultimately produced a treasure trove of information and some remarkable personal relationships. By this time, I knew the names and hometowns of all the survivors. Through a combination of phone calls to possible descendants (for typically less common surnames) and to American Legion and VFW posts and local newspaper editors, descendants of all but Mario Muzzi and Feodor Sok were found. Fortunately, Joseph Kornacki's grandson, Dave Kornacki, and Otis Merrithew's daughter and grandson, Lorraine and Jim Fallon, were among the first. Dave, in addition to providing detailed information on his grandfather, became a tireless partner in the project, doing invaluable research and later setting up a website for "The Other Sixteen" for which he wrote much of the commentary. That website helped lead to the discoveries of other descendants. The Fallons also were indispensable, having preserved all of Otis Merrithew's papers, including detailed correspondence with Col. Buxton and others that never before had been made public. As the chief "troublemaker," Otis had been the most persistent member of the sixteen in gaining recognition for the other members of the patrol. James Gregory discusses the correspondence that Jim Fallon provided in detail in the book with insightful comments.

I was also able to track down Percy Beardsley's nephew Natc (the namesake of Percy's father) and son Don in Massachusetts. They shared many stories about Uncle Percy. The town of Roxbury actually hosted a day in Percy's honor, which they attended. Sadly, both died in the last few years. Percy married late in life and never had children. His wife, Louise, sold the family home in the 1970s to David Shaber and his wife, who used it as a retreat where David, who was a renowned screenwriter, wrote the screenplay for such hits as *The Warriors, Nighthawks, Rollover,* and *The Hunt for Red October.* I visited Mrs. Shaber last year at her home, which was then for sale, hoping against the odds that the steamer trunk pictured in one of the 1960s local newspaper articles about Percy would still be in the attic. In the photos, it contained his uniform and .45 sidearm from the war. Alas, it was long gone. But memories and stories of the Beardsleys were not.

Patrick Donohue's great niece was still in his hometown of Lawrence, Massachusetts. James describes the poignant effort, ultimately successful, to find Patrick's medals. Through the efforts of his niece, Pat Waters, Patrick, who had a particularly difficult time adjusting to civilian life after the war, was finally recognized in his hometown as the hero he was with a town square named after him.

Michael Sacina's great niece was living in New York City where Michael spent his entire life after emigrating from Italy. In a biography she wrote for The Other Sixteen website about her great uncle, she described him as a quiet, unassuming man. She did not recall him ever talking about the war. This memory seems consistent with his behavior in other respects and is typical of so many of the sixteen men. He never responded to the invitation to the 1929 War College Event, and he did not participate in the discussions about the 1941 movie. Despite Michael's reluctance to discuss the war, one of the other members of Company G, Ruggero Barone, had heard about Michael's role. We were contacted by Ruggero's son and granddaughter. Ruggero had told them about his part in the October 8, 1918, battle where he was wounded. Ruggero insisted that Michael Sacina had played a significant role in it—and never received acknowledgment. Joseph, his son, who has since died, showed us his father's nickel-plated revolver which he carried throughout the war. Ruggero was an American success story. Living on Sullivan Street in New York's Little Italy at the time he was drafted, he went on to drive for and then eventually became a partial owner of the famed Green Line Bus Company in New York.

Descendants of George Washington Wills and Thomas Johnson proved difficult to find, perhaps partly because of their common surnames. A lawyer friend in Philadelphia tracked down probate court records for George Wills, who died at the Philadelphia Naval Hospital. Reporters in their respective hometowns of Philadelphia and Lynchburg helped by writing articles in the local paper after I contacted editors at their paper and sent packets of information. The articles created a great deal of interest. Readers responded with tips on relatives. George Wills's grandson (George III) and his wife Carol connected me with George Wills's son (George II), who was still living in the extremely modest south Philadelphia neighborhood where he had grown up and where his father scavenged for his livelihood at the old Philadelphia City dump (the area is now the site of the National Football League and Major League Baseball sports stadiums). It was also where his brother had been incinerated as a boy in a freak accident after being soaked in oil. In a prominent place on the wall of his living room was a portrait of his father in his World War I uniform. George II was well versed in the York story, remembering the names of Sgt. Early and some of the other men. He also was adamant about the role his father and the other men played but for which they were not recognized.

Thomas Johnson even now remains something of an enigma. He had moved from Lynchburg to Denison, Texas, in the late 1920s with his mother, older brother, and three of his sister's orphans. Denison has two long-time funeral directors. It turns out one of them had buried Thomas and was able to find the file for me. It contained an obituary from the *Denison Herald* for Thomas, who died at the age of 66 on September 23,

1961. The short, but elegiac and haunting obituary mentioned no family, career, or other personal matters—only his involvement with the battle for which Alvin York became famous. It reads as follows:

> A man who knew the fierce sounds of battle beside Sgt. Alvin York in the Argonne Forest during World War I was laid to rest in a quiet plot at the north edge of Fairview Cemetery Tuesday.
>
> Thomas Gibb Johnson, 66, received little recognition as one of the 10 men who lived through the fierce battle in which his group cut down a German machine gun battalion. His role in the battle came to light when the movie on Sgt. York's life was made. The Herald found Johnson living here quietly nursing nerves shattered by the war.
>
> Rev. Bill Davis spoke at the simple but impressive graveside services for Johnson, taking note of his retiring nature and his contentment to let others take credit for his brief brush with glory.
>
> Six Word War I veterans served as pallbearers for [the] flag-draped coffin. They were: Ralph Dunbar, Arthur Fleming, George Johnson, Allen Gray, Joe Donald and Tracy Leis.
>
> Hartley Edwards, Denison's famous World War I bugler, sounded taps, and after a few words of prayer, the three dozen mourners began drifting away, leaving the body of Denison's unsung World War I hero to its eternal rest.

Chris DuMond, a reporter for *The Lynchburg News and Advance* who took a special interest in Johnson, wrote a long article about him and was able to locate his two great nieces. They had not known of his role in the war and were delighted to discover it when they contacted me.

Despite several leads that looked promising, we were not able to find a descendant of Mario Muzzi. Although he had married, it appears that he had never had children. Wounded in the battle on October 8, 1918, he retired after many years of working for the Nabisco bakery in New York City to his hometown of Civita di Bagnoregio in Italy. He died there at the age of 90 in April 1978, the last of the "Other Sixteen." Perhaps living in Civita contributed to his longevity by keeping him fit—Civita is a hilltop village not far from Rome which is accessed exclusively by a narrow pedestrian bridge.

Despite several promising leads, we never found a confirmed descendant of Feodor Sok who was one of the three patrol members from upstate New York. James Gregory has found some information that may prove helpful in locating one of his relatives.

Even though my original intention was to find descendants of the survivors of the patrol since presumably survivors would have lived to tell their version of the battle, it became clear that others who saw battle that day could add to our understanding of the men involved, the battle and its impact.

Eventually, through a variety of sources, including more newspaper articles and some referrals from Michael Kelly, we were able to locate and speak with descendants of five of the six men killed in action that day: Maryan Dymowski, Murray Savage, Carl Swanson, Fred Wareing, and Ralph Weiler. From them came photographs, postcards, newspaper clippings, obituaries. and more. Murray Savage's great-niece, who still lives in Canandaigua, New York where he lived, shared photos of Murray in front of the local courthouse on the day he left for the Army looking determined and maybe a bit anxious dressed in suit, tie, and cap; a photo of him later in uniform; a letter he wrote from Camp Gordon, Georgia, during basic training thanking everyone at home for Christmas gifts and talking about Army life there; and, finally, a letter returning to his sister mail undeliverable due to his death.

Carl Swanson's great-niece had photos of Carl, who was from Jamestown, also in upstate New York. No letters were located, but stories of Carl were passed down through the family, including the story that when he went off to Camp Gordon, he was tall and stooped. After basic training he came home for a visit and was "straight as an arrow." She still has five 1905 Indian Head pennies he gave to his youngest sister, her mother, before shipping out.

Maryan Dymowski's great-niece, who lives near Trenton, New Jersey, where Maryan lived, sent photos of him—pre-Army with friends at the beach—and of Company G at Camp Gordon, as well as a copy of his obituary. On quiet nights, she said she remembers her mother, who was Maryan's youngest sister, reading and rereading George Pattullo's article because it mentioned Maryan and the battle, and crying. With help from a Polish friend, she is in the process of translating Maryan's letters home from the Army which were passed down to her.

According to his great-nephew, Fred Wareing's death was a terrible blow to his widowed mother and youngest brother who idolized him.

His youngest brother spoke of Fred on many occasions and had not fully gotten over his brother's death. Fred's mother, Flora, had a dream one night in which Fred came to her in uniform and said "it's alright ma." The following day she received notice that he had been killed.

We also contacted Col. Buxton's grandson, Ned Buxton, who has written a yet unpublished memoir of his grandfather. As James details in his book, in his later years Col. Buxton tried to help Otis and the others get recognition for their role in the battle. In speaking with Ned, he told me that over the years, Col. Buxton increasingly came to believe that the other men played a more significant role in the battle than they were given credit.

And of course there is Lt. Kirby Stewart, platoon leader of Company G, who was awarded the DSC posthumously. He was the only platoon leader who was single and volunteered to lead the attack that day. Running across 500 yards of hilly, open terrain, he was hit but continued to rally his troops before being fatally shot in the head. In 2008, I tracked down Kirby's nephew and namesake in Bradenton, Florida, with the help of the commander of the Bradenton American Legion Post 24, named after Lt. Stewart in 1920. Bradenton was Lt. Stewart's hometown. My oldest son and I visited him there at his invitation. Like Percy Beardsley's ancestors, one of Kirby's forebears living in Georgia had fought in the American Revolution. Lt. Stewart was also a distant cousin of Teddy Roosevelt. The younger Kirby shared photos, letters, and many family memories

Kirby Stewart. Courtesy of Rosalyn F. Way, on behalf of all living relatives of Lt. Kirby P. Stewart.

of his uncle. One of the letters described Company G taking the town of Norroy in September 1918, a subject discussed in the Skeyhill book. Also included was a clipping describing how, on October 2, 1918, Lt. Stewart's girlfriend, Rosalyn Byrd, whom he met when he was at Camp Gordon, plucked a dozen four leaf clovers from a Georgia curbside, put them in an envelope and wrote, "I hope they bring you good luck." He never received them. His family was notified of his death by telegram at their Bradenton home the morning of November 11—Armistice Day. Rosalyn later married Stewart's younger brother. The younger Kirby died in December 2017.

In 2008, we organized several meetings of descendants in Massachusetts. It was at the first of these meetings, in March 2008, that the name "The Other Sixteen" was suggested. Then, in April 2009, Dave Kornacki and I traveled to France at the invitation of the Nolan and Kelly group who were completing their dig at the site of the battle. There, we were able to walk what is most likely the same route on which my great uncle, Sgt. Early, led that seventeen-man patrol on October 8, 1918—the dream of a nine-year-old me clipping and saving from the Register that newspaper article. Dave and I also visited the graves of the four members of the "Other Sixteen" interred in the American Meuse-Argonne military cemetery at Romagne, France.

James Gregory and Steven Girard contacted Dave Kornacki and me in 2018 after seeing an earlier video of our descendants group, which included my cousin Karen (Bernie's granddaughter) and the former mayor of Hamden, Connecticut, John Carusone. By then, our project had been mostly on hold for a while. Career and family obligations were partly to blame for the delay, but also a certain degree of uncertainty about the next steps and the difficulty accessing other resources held us back. James Gregory, with Steven's help, persuaded us that he had the capability and energy to take a fresh look at what actually happened on that cold, foggy morning near Chatel-Chéhéry on October 8, 1918. In addition to reviewing all the information we provided, he and Steven used resources obtained through their military connections that we were unable to tap. Somewhat incredibly, we located the original affidavits that had eluded every author heretofore. Some had even concluded that the affidavits may not have existed. Through careful analysis, James was able to demonstrate what seems now to be their obvious defects. James further demonstrates, through careful step-by-step reconstruction of the battle sequence, conclusively I think, that the legendary "turkey shoot" never happened. Of course, Alvin York himself finally admitted to the same in a newspaper interview that, amazingly, seems to have been ignored by all the commentators. James also makes a strong case that Otis Merrithew remained in command of the returning patrol.

Working with James has rekindled my interest and, I think it's safe to say, that of Dave Kornacki and Jim Fallon in our project. Recently, I decided to expand research to other members of Company G. Three of them are Connecticut men. Rufus Walter Bishop was one of the first to see the survivors return from the battle. I discovered that he wrote extensively about his experience in both letters and a diary. In 1920, Bishop wrote to his local paper to correct what he perceived as a misconception regarding Sgt. Early's role. Modern travelers on the Connecticut Turnpike (Interstate 95) will notice billboards for the Bishop Orchards store, a well-known locale for generations here run by Rufus Walter's descendants.

Sgt. Walter Stapf was of German heritage and lived in Seymour, Connecticut, ten minutes from where I now sit writing this chapter. He was another Company G man. He is honored at the local Seymour American Legion Post. Sgt. Stapf was severely wounded in the attack on October 8, 1918, and died a week or so later in hospital. The Legion commander is helping to find a relative. As with some of the other men, some of Sgt. Stapf's letters were published in the local paper as was his obituary, which seems to be missing from the archives. I discovered that every day on the way to work for almost thirty years I have been driving by the cemetery where Stapf is buried and his family home. His grave is on a hillside on one side of the Naugatuck River, and the home is on the opposite side, each visible from the other place.

There is also John Jesse Bushnell, originally from picturesque New Milford, Connecticut, less than a half hour from Percy's hometown of Roxbury. John also was wounded on October 8, 1918, in the attack. According to his son, Jack, he moved to Massachusetts after the war when he saw no further opportunity in tobacco farming in Litchfield County, Connecticut. In the familiar refrain for most of these men, his son described him as a quiet man who rarely spoke of the war. One thing he remembered clearly, though, was that John believed the York legend was "a lot to do about nothing." Jack sent me photos and articles of his father in uniform and when he was awarded a Purple Heart in a ceremony on Veterans Day 1985, sixty-seven years after he was wounded.

And, too, there are Elijah Loyd Ellis of Experiment, Georgia, and Albert Bendic Dravland of North Dakota. Ellis is the man who, in 1935, following a radio broadcast of the American Legion's action to obtain the Medal of Honor for Sgt. Early, wrote to the Connecticut newspaper, the *Hartford Courant*, to describe how he had helped carry the wounded Early to an aid station and how he was sure Early had later died from his severe wounds. Aroused to action by the report, Ellis wrote in 1935 that Sgt. Early "certainly deserves more credit than anyone else." Ellis's grandson told me his grandfather was so impressed with the heroism of his friend Albert Dravland (another Company G man) that day as a stretcher bearer that he named his first son after him—"Dravland." Albert Dravland also won the DSC for his heroism that day as a World War I version of Desmond Doss. In addition, Albert maintained a close friendship with Rufus Walter Bishop for many years after the war, with the men even visiting each other in Connecticut and North Dakota.

My conversations with descendants make clear that now, more than a century after the battle, these men and their stories are still cherished by their families. For many of them, the battle was *the* defining event in their lives, for better or worse.

So where does all of this leave us and our project? Is the case definitively settled beyond any reasonable doubt as to who did exactly what on October 8, 1918? No, and it probably never will be. But in the calculus of heroism, if there is one, it is certainly clearer with James Gregory's book that the "Other Sixteen" played a greater role in the battle, and Alvin York a lesser role, than history has recognized.

Was Alvin York any more of a hero than Sgt. Early who took over as leader of the suicide mission after Lt. Stewart was killed and skillfully led his group of seventeen men in a flanking maneuver without the loss of a single man and capturing close to a hundred Germans? Clearly, without Kirby Stewart and Bernard Early—both of whom were awarded the DSC for their actions that day—there would have been no York legend. Or Otis Merrithew who remained in charge of the patrol but had to wait 50 years for his Silver Star? Or Albert Dravland? Or any of the others?

Why is Alvin York in the pantheon of American military heroes, while Stewart, Early, and all the others are mere footnotes in history whose roles are known mostly only by family? Could it be that York simply had better publicists?

Or perhaps Percy Beardsley had it right all along. When asked why the other survivors allowed York to receive sole credit, Percy said "Well, York was always a pretty good fellow for letting everyone know how good he was. He never missed a chance."[3]

I join Steven Girard in hoping that James Gregory's book will set the record straight and serve as a catalyst for the long-delayed recognition of the "Other Sixteen" and reconsideration of what happened that day.

Robert V. D'Angelo Jr.
Woodbridge, Connecticut

Appendix 1:

Letter from G. Edward Buxton to Gen. George B. Duncan, April 22, 1932

ROOM 1028
40 WORTH STREET
NEW YORK CITY

April 22, 1932

General George B. Duncan
450 West Second Street,
Lexington, Kentucky

Dear General Duncan:-

First, let me say to you how pleased I was to learn of Julian Lindsey's promotion and my appreciation of the fact that it was wholly due to your interest in his behalf. He writes me recently that he went over to see you his first weekend from Camp Knox.

Second, I wanted to add a few comments on the matter of the recommendation concerning Corporal Cutting - certainly not with the idea of asking you to reverse your decision, but only to make certain that you are in full possession of the facts. The investigation, made first in the 328th Infantry and subsequently by me at your direction, was in some ways unfortunate for Sergeant Early and Corporal Cutting, both of whom were in the hospital and never rejoined the regiment. It is true that I asked many questions about both of them, as my Sergeant-Major, Safferman, can witness. The survivors were not a very articulate lot, and, as is often the case under emergency conditions, had little idea of what happened to anybody except themselves, or what their comrades were doing. Sergeant York alone was able to tell a vivid, continuous story; and there was never any doubt in my mind that the burden of the fire fight fell upon his shoulders. It struck me at the time that Early, the senior in command, led the reconnaissance skilfully, estimated the situation and made a very important and distinguished decision when he ordered the attack against an unknown force which he must have believed would greatly outnumber his own. He heard voices and saw men moving in the brush at the foot of the hill and made a vigorous surprise attack. Early received the first surrender of the group at the

foot of the hill (about 60 men), stopped his own men
from firing, and was then robbed of the fruits of his
victory by the surprise fire from the hillside overhead. Early was properly rewarded at the Army War
College affair in Washington a few years ago. You
will remember that I wrote you recommending the D. S. C.
for Early shortly after I left the service, and you forwarded the same with approval to the War Department.
This letter was ignored until the Washington York party,
when I was asked to put the substance of my letter in
affidavit form, and the D. S. C. was conferred upon
Early during the exercises. York fully concurred in
this award.

I have never seen Cutting until he
appeared at this meeting, filled with a sense of having
been unfairly ignored in the general publicity. I
was able to avert a very embarrassing situation for the
officers in charge of the show by getting Cutting one
side and listening to his story, examining the scars in
his left arm--all flesh wounds. He asserts stoutly, and
is supported by the four or five others among the survivors who talked with me, that he used a revolver with
his right hand and fired aimed shots from where he knelt
on the ground. He believes that he was the non-commissioned officer in command when Early went down and out,
and Early supports this statement. Captain Danforth is
inclined to regard York and Cutting as probably of equal
grade,--both were Acting Corporals. Savage, the third
non-commissioned officer, was killed. Cutting insists
that he took charge equally with York in bringing out the
prisoners. Sergeant Parsons, their platoon sergeant,
noticed, when the party of prisoners returned to the
company on the other side of the hill, Cutting walking
on the left flank, a German pistol in his right hand
and the blood running down his left arm. Parsons says
that Cutting showed him the pistol, and said, "I got
what I went for." Parsons states he grabbed Cutting and
insisted that he go to the dressing station at once to
have his arm cared for.

I must confess that I have taken
an additional interest in this whole matter in order to
silence some of the efforts to discredit Sergeant York.
There is a great gulf between the Medal of Honor and
the Distinguished Service Cross, which makes clear the
difference in achievement between York and Cutting.
Of course, none of us who were not eye witnesses will
ever know exactly what happened, except that Early was
responsible for the attack, and York for winning the
fire fight. No doubt, we would have been justified in

giving Division Citations to every member of the little
party, although some acted better than others. Cutting
could, I think, easily persuade some audiences that he
lost his chance for reward because he was not present
at the investigation in France, and because his comrades
failed to bring him adequately to the attention of the
division authorities. He says that he permitted the
matter to rest for several years without asking for an
investigation because he had enlisted in the Army under
a false name--his real name being Otis B. Merrithew.
This, he asserts, was for no dishonorable reasons, but
for personal reasons.

        Please write me frankly whether any
of these comments are new to you, and second, whether
you advise against my forwarding the affidavits with a
statement that I have no personal knowledge of what
took place, but believe that the survivors are sincere
in their statements.

        Between ourselves, I cannot make up
my mind whether Sergeant York regards Cutting as a boaster
or whether he expressed his whole viewpoint when he told
me that he didn't know what anybody in the detachment did
except himself, that he was too busy in the fire fight
and that so far as he knows Cutting may have done what
he says he did. Sergeant York told me that he saw Cutting
with the other survivors after the fight at the foot of
the hill and that Cutting came out with the rest of the
column.
        I am sorry to inflict this long
blast upon you, but do want to make certain that we
settle this thing right before we drop it forever.
For some reason, all these men have kept writing me, and
except for a certain sense of obligation to men who once
served under me, I would have been glad to be free of it
long ago.

        I am now in New York about five
days a week. My address is Room 1028, 40 Worth Street,
New York City; telephone number Worth 2, 0463. When you
come to New York, as I understand you do occasionally, do
not fail to give me a chance to spend an evening with you.
With warmest regards and respects to you and Mrs. Duncan,

        Faithfully yours,

G. Edward Buxton.d

        Ned Buxton.

Appendix 2:

Letter from Early, Merrithew, Beardsley, Donohue, Kornacki, and Sok to The Boston Globe, July 14, 1941

July 14, 1941

17 Whitney Street

Chestnut Hill, Mass.
Editor, Boston Globe,
Washington Street,
Boston, Mass

Dear Sir,

In regards to the York Motion Picture that is now playing to a full house in New York and is about to open in Boston, I wish to inform you that none of the survivors are in agreement with Warner Brothers' or with Sergeant York's version of what really happened "over there" on that memorial morning of Oct. 8, 1918 in the Argonne Forest.

We, the undersigned, will solemnly swear that, to the best of our ability we never recall signing any affidavit in regards to York's heroism that morning. That would be against our grain as we always had Sergeant York figured out to be "yellow" and not a conscientious objector; we recall one morning as we were to go "over the top", York went stark mad with fear. He jumped up on top of the parapet and started to holler, "I want to go home, For God's sake why isn't this war over."

We all recall this incident to be true and from then on we knew for a fact that York was "yellow". Sgt. Early rushed up to him (York) and pushed his automatic pistol at his head and said, "if you don't shut up, I'll blow your brains out." As we all knew that York was exposing our whereabouts to the enemy. As Early reported this to our Co. Commander later he said that Early would have been justified in "blowing York's brains out."

In regards to our signing any affidavits that is a lie. He has nothing signed by Sergeant Early or by Corporal Cutting, or Merrithew which was his right name. Our Division Historian claims that the other surviving privates signed affidavits supporting York's claims which we claim not be the truth.

We will admit, though, that we though we were signing too many papers at the time and thought that we were being well-clothed by our supply Sergeant. Every other day we were being asked to sign for a suit of underwear or for a pair of stockings. We knew what we had done that morning "over there" and there should have been enough glory to go all around but we were surprised when we found out later that York was getting all the Decorations and we were being left out in the cold.

It took Sgt. York twenty-two years to get up enough courage to be so bold as to state that he should get all the credit for what we really did "over there".

There must have been a reason for this and the public know that reason. York never dared showed his face in New Haven (where Early lives). He came once to Boston but he never knew that Merrithew lived there and he has never appeared in Boston since that time. Why?

He must have had plenty of offers as we all know that it took him twenty-two years to accept Jesse L. Lasky's offer out of thousands of other which he undoubtedly had to turn down.

Now, the point is this: why did he wait for Lasky's offer? Were the others too small to gamble with? Or was he afraid of us (the survivors) telling the truth?

We, the undersigned, think that York should be made to tell the truth at this time and be made to give "credit where credit is due."

For more about Sgt. York, contact any of the men that were with him in that famous battle.

Sergeant Bernard Early
Corp. Otis B. Merrithew
Privates Percy Beardsley
Patrick Donohue
Joseph Kornacki
Fred Sok

Notes

Introduction

1. This story is an amalgamation of several books and the movie *Sergeant York*. It represents the generally accepted myth of Alvin York and as such is not quoted from any specific source.

Chapter 1

1. Bernard Early, serial number 2559, no. 313, Precinct 7, City of New Haven, Connecticut, United States, Selective Service System, *World War I Selective Service System Draft Registration Cards, 1917–1918*. Washington, DC: National Archives and Records Administration. M1509, 4,582 rolls. Henceforth, shortened to WWI Draft Registration Cards.

2. Murray Savage, serial number 46, no. 46, Precinct 1, Ontario, New York, WWI Draft Registration Cards; Murray Savage, *New York State Abstracts of World War I Military Service, 1917–1919*, Adjutant General's Office. Series B0808, New York State Archives, Albany, NY.

3. Letter from Elizabeth Savage, Burial File of Corporal Murray Savage, Box 4297, RG 92, Records of the Graves Registration Services, National Archive and Records Administration, College Park, MD.

4. *Pilgrimage for the Mothers and Widows of Soldiers, Sailors, and Marines of the American Forces Now Interred in the Cemeteries of Europe* (Washington, DC: US Government Printing Office, 1930), 208.

5. Michael Kelly, *Hero on the Western Front: Discovering Alvin York's WWI Battlefield* (Philadelphia, PA: Frontline Books, 2018), 288, 301–322.

6. William Cutting (Otis Merrithew), serial number 3162, no. 853, Precinct 8, Bridgeport, Connecticut, WWI Draft Registration Cards; William Cutting, Military Service Record, State of Connecticut; Interview with Jimmy Fallon, December 27, 2019.

7. Kelly, *Hero on the Western Front*, 304.

8. Carl Swanson, serial number 3587, no. 765, Precinct 2–6, Jamestown, NY, WWI Draft Registration Cards; Carl Swanson, *New York State Abstracts of World War I Military Service, 1917–1919*, Adjutant General's Office. Series B0808, New York State Archives, Albany, NY.

9. Theador Sok (Feodor Sok), serial number 3536, no. 535, Precinct 3–4, Buffalo, NY, WWI Draft Registration Cards; Feodor Sok, *New York State Abstracts of World War I Military Service, 1917–1919*, Adjutant General's Office. Series B0808, New York State Archives, Albany, NY

10. Fred Wareing, serial number 12062, no. 382, Precinct 24, Ward 6, New Bedford, MA, WWI Draft Registration Cards.

11. *Pilgrimage for the Mothers and Widows of Soldiers, Sailors, and Marines of the American Forces Now Interred in the Cemeteries of Europe* (Washington, DC: US Government Printing Office, 1930), 114.

12. Robert D'Angelo, interview with James Gregory, March 15, 2019.

13. George Wills, serial number 2966, no. 150, Precinct 26, Philadelphia, PA, WWI Draft Registration Cards.

14. Thirteenth Census of the United States, 1910 (NARA microfilm publication T624, 1,178 rolls). Records of the Bureau of the Census, Record Group 29. National Archives, Washington, DC; Joseph Kornotski (Kornacki), serial number 2536, no. 283, Precinct B, Ward 3, Holyoke, MA, WWI Draft Registration Cards.

15. There is a discrepancy with his birthdate. His US passport application and World War II draft registration give his birthdate as October 8, while his World War I draft registration and US Social Security index give his birthdate as October 18.

16. Mario Muzzi, serial number 1848, no. 74, Precinct 29, New York, NY, WWI Draft Registration Cards; Mario Muzzi, *New York State Abstracts of World War I Military Service, 1917–1919*, Adjutant General's Office. Series B0808, New York State Archives, Albany, NY.

17. Kelly, *Hero on the Western Front*, 308.

18. Maryan Dymowski, serial number 2319, no. 815, Stratford, CT, WWI Draft Registration Cards; *Pilgrimage for the Mothers and Widows of Soldiers, Sailors, and Marines of the American Forces Now Interred in the Cemeteries of Europe* (Washington, DC: US Government Printing Office, 1930), 180.

19. *1920*, Census Place: *Queens Assembly District 3, Queens, New York*, Roll: *T625_1231*, Page *7B*, Enumeration District: *174, 1920 United States Federal Census*; Michael Sacina, serial number 337, no. 197, Precinct 63, New York, NY, WWI Draft Registration Cards.

20. Patrick Donohue, *1910 Census*, Census Place: *Lawrence Ward 3, Essex, Massachusetts*, Roll: *T624_583*, Page *33A*, Enumeration District: *1937*, FHL microfilm: *1374596, United States Federal Census*; Patrick Donohue, serial number 4480, no. 113, Precinct 8, Ward 3, Lawrence, MA, WWI Draft Registration Cards.

21. Percy Beardsley, serial number 407, no. 1, Roxbury, CT, WWI Draft Registration Cards.

22. Ralph Weiler, serial number 2397, no. 37, Ward 2, Hanover, PA, WWI Draft Registration Cards; Ralph Weiler, *Pennsylvania, U.S., World War I Veterans Service and Compensation Files, 1917–1919, 1934–1948*, World War I Veterans Service and Compensation File, 1934–1948. RG 19, Series 19.91, Pennsylvania Historical and Museum Commission, Harrisburg, PA; "Another Soldier from Hanover is Killed in France," *The Evening Sun*, November 22, 1918.

23. *Pilgrimage for the Mothers and Widows of Soldiers, Sailors, and Marines of the American Forces Now Interred in the Cemeteries of Europe* (Washington, DC: US Government Printing Office, 1930), 276.

24. Thomas Gibbs Johnson, serial number 1197, no. 159, Precinct 1, Lynchburg, VA, WWI Draft Registration Cards; SS *Martha Washington* transport log, *US Army Transport Service Arriving and Departing Passenger Lists, 1910–1939*, Records of the Office of the Quartermaster General, 1774–1985, Record Group 92. The National Archives at College Park, MD.

25. William Wine, serial number 2128, no. 107, Ward 23, Philadelphia, WWI Draft Registration Cards.

26. Alvin C. York, *Sergeant York: His Own Life Story and War Diary*, edited by Tom Skeyhill (Garden City, NY: Doubleday, Doran, 1928), 286.

27. George Duncan, *Reminiscences of the World* War, George Brand Duncan Papers, 1882–1948, University of Kentucky Special Collections Research Center, 152.

28. Sandra Turner, Sergeant *Alvin C. York: The Making of a Hero and Legend*, (CreateSpace Independent Publishing Platform, 2015), 21.

29. Joseph Cummings Chase, "Corporal York, General Pershing, and Others," *World's Work* 37 (April 1919): 648.

30. Telegram from George Pattullo to Colonel Gordon Johnston, January 26, 1919, in Alvin C. York, US Army Service Record, National Personnel Record Center, St. Louis, MO.

31. George Seldes, *Tell the Truth and Run* (New York: Greenburg, 1953), 40–41.

32. George Pattullo, "The Second Elder Gives Battle," *The Saturday Evening Post*, April 26, 1919: 3.

33. Robert Bellah, "Civil Religion in America," *Daedalus* 96, no. 1 (Winter 1967): 1–21.

34. David D. Lee, *Sergeant York: An American Hero* (Lexington: University Press of Kentucky, 1985), 58.

35. Pattullo, "The Second Elder Gives Battle," 73.

36. G. Edward Buxton Jr, *Official History of the 82nd Division, AEF, 1917–1919*, (Indianapolis, IN: Bobbs-Merrill, 1919), 60–62.

37. Samuel K. Cowan, *Sergeant York and His People* (New York: Funk and Wagnalls, 1922), 12–13.

38. Ibid., 122.

39. John Perry, *Sgt. York: His Life, Legacy, & Legend* (Nashville, TN: Broadman & Holman, 1997), 161.

40. Alvin C. York, "The Diary of Sergeant York," *Liberty Magazine*, July 14, 1928, 9.

41. Alvin C. York, *Sergeant York: His Own Life Story and War Diary*, edited by Tom Skeyhill (Garden City, NY: Doubleday, Doran, 1928), 240–244.

42. Jeff Brownrigg, *Anzac Cove to Hollywood: The Story of Tom Skeyhill, Master of Deception* (Spit Junction, NSW: Anchor Books Australia, 2010), 175.

43. York, *Sergeant York*, 226.

44. Lee, *Sergeant York*, 96.

45. "Sergt York Gets Great Reception," *The Boston Globe*, January 29, 1920; "Denies York Claim to Argonne Glory," *The Springfield Daily Republican*, October 2, 1929.

46. Tom Skeyhill, *Sergeant York: Last of the Long Hunters* (Philadelphia: Winston, 1930), 7, 183, 185.

47. Ibid, 1.

48. Harry R. Stringer, *Heroes All! A Compendium of the Names and Official Citations of the Soldiers and Citizens of the United States and of her Allies who were Decorated by the American Government for Exceptional Heroism and Conspicuous Service Above and Beyond the Call of Duty in the War with Germany, 1917–1919* (Washington, DC: Fassett, 1919), 26, 429.

49. Lee, *Sergeant York*, 92.

Chapter 2

1. From this point to footnote 51, the written information is derived from the *History of the Three Hundred and Twenty-Eighth Regiment of Infantry, Eighty-Second Division*. Rather than fill the pages with footnotes of the same source, I will cite at the end with the appropriate page numbers except in cases of direct quotes.

2. Scott Chandler, *History of the Three Hundred and Twenty-Eighth Regiment of Infantry, Eighty-Second Division* (Atlanta: Foote and Davies, 1920), 9.

3. *U.S., Army Transport Service Arriving and Departing Passenger Lists, 1910–1939*, The National Archives at College Park; College Park, Maryland; Record Group Title: *Records of the Office of the Quartermaster General, 1774–1985*; Record Group Number: *92*; Roll or Box Number: *589*.

4. Chandler, *History of the Three Hundred and Twenty-Eighth Regiment*, 17.

5. Ibid., 7–44.

Chapter 3

1. G. Edward Buxton Jr., *Official History of the 82nd Division AEF, 1917–1919*, (Indianapolis, IN: Bobbs-Merrill, 1919), 87.

2. Scott Chandler, *History of the Three Hundred and Twenty-Eighth Regiment of Infantry, Eighty-Second Division* (Atlanta: Foote and Davies, 1920), 59.

3. *Regimental Special Orders No. 134,* November 3, 1918, NARA, St. Louis, MO.

4. Chandler, *History of the Three Hundred and Twenty-Eighth Regiment of Infantry*, 63.

5. Alvin C. York, *Sergeant York: His Own Life Story and War Diary*, edited by Tom Skeyhill (Garden City, NY: Doubleday, Doran, 1928), 286.

6. Distinguished Service Cross Affidavit, October 23, 1918, in Alvin C. York, U.S. Army Service Record, National Personnel Record Center, St. Louis, Missouri.

7. Memorandum for Major Smith, in Alvin C. York, U.S. Army Service Record, National Personnel Record Center, St. Louis, Missouri.

8. Buxton, *Official History of the 82nd Division*, iii.

9. York, *Sergeant York*, 249–257.

10. Michael Kelly claimed that Buxton's statements could no longer be found as source documents, so he had to use Skeyhill's manuscript draft to cite them in full. Buxton's statements do not appear in York's official service file, supporting the idea that these were part of Buxton's research rather than an official investigation.

11. Letter from Edward Buxton to George Duncan, April 22, 1932, George Brand Duncan Papers, 1882–1948, University of Kentucky Special Collections Research Center.

12. Frederic Kelly, "New Haven's Forgotten Hero: Should Bernard Early Share Alvin York's World War I Honors?" *The New Haven Register*, New Haven, CT, November 8, 1964.

13. Harry R. Stringer, *Heroes All! A Compendium of the Names and Official Citations of the Soldiers and Citizens of the United States and of her Allies who were Decorated by the American Government for Exceptional Heroism and Conspicuous Service Above and Beyond the Call of Duty in the War with Germany, 1917–1919* (Washington, DC: Fassett Publishing Co., 1919), 2, 4.

14. Distinguished Service Cross Affidavit, October 23, 1918, in Alvin C. York, U.S. Army Service Record, National Personnel Record Center, St. Louis, MO.

15. Sandra Turner, Sergeant ,*Alvin C. York: The Making of a Hero and Legend,* (CreateSpace Independent Publishing Platform, 2015), 21.

16. Michael Kelly, *Hero on the Western Front: Discovering Alvin York's WWI Battlefield* (Philadelphia: Frontline Books, 2018), 64.

17. "Then and Now," *The American Legion Monthly,* Vol 2, No. 5, May 1927, 57

18. Medal of Honor Affidavit, February 6, 1919, in Alvin C. York, U.S. Army Service Record, National Personnel Record Center, St. Louis, MO.

19. Cablegram from General Pershing, March 14, 1919, in Alvin C. York, U.S. Army Service Record, National Personnel Record Center, St. Louis, MO.

20. Medal of Honor Affidavit, February 6, 1919, in Alvin C. York, U.S. Army Service Record, National Personnel Record Center, St. Louis, MO.

21. Letter from G. E. Buxton to Otis Merrithew, October 8, 1929, Jimmy Fallon Collection.

22. Affidavit of Percy Beardsley and George Wills, February 21, 1919, in Alvin C. York, U.S. Army Service Record, National Personnel Record Center, St. Louis, MO.

23. Letter from Edward Buxton to George Duncan, April 22, 1932, George Brand Duncan Papers, 1882–1948, University of Kentucky Special Collections Research Center.

24. Alvin C. York, *Sergeant York: His Own Life Story and War Diary*, edited by Tom Skeyhill (Garden City, NY: Doubleday, Doran, 1928), 251–256.

25. Letter to Editor of the *Boston Globe*, July 14, 1941, Warner Bros. Archive, Archives at USC Libraries, USC, Los Angeles, CA; and Jimmy Fallon Collection.

26. Chandler, *History of the Three Hundred and Twenty-Eighth Regiment of Infantry*, 9.

27. "World War I Draft Registration Cards, 1917–1918," digital image, Theodor Sok registration, serial number 3536, no. 535, Draft Board 3, City of Buffalo, NY; citing World War I Selective Service System Draft Registration Cards, 1917–1918, NARA microfilm publication.

28. "World War I Draft Registration Cards, 1917–1918," digital image, Joseph Kornotski registration, serial number 2536, no. 283, Ward 3, City of Holyoke, MA; citing World War I Selective Service System Draft Registration Cards, 1917–1918, NARA microfilm publication.

29. "Konotski in Affidavit Denies Crediting York," *Springfield Republican*, October 9, 1929.

30. Distinguished Service Cross Affidavit, October 23, 1918, in Alvin C. York, U.S. Army Service Record, National Personnel Record Center, St. Louis, Missouri.

31. Recommendations from Richard Wetherill, Julian Lindsey, W. K. Merritt, E. A. Burkhalter, Bertrand Cox, J. M. Tillman and George Duncan, February 7, 1919, in Alvin C. York, U.S. Army Service Record, National Personnel Record Center, St. Louis, MO; Frank C. Phillips, "Signal Corps Photograph 49192," National Archives.

32. Recommendation from Richard Wetherill to George Duncan, February

7, 1919, in Alvin C. York, U.S. Army Service Record, National Personnel Record Center, St. Louis, MO.

33. Buxton, *Official History of the 82nd Division*, 62.

34. Statement of Otis B. Merrithew sworn to by Patrick J. Donohue, October 31, 1929, Jimmy Fallon Collection.

35. Letter from Robert Davis to Carleton Collins, March 21, 1927, in Alvin C. York, U.S. Army Service Record, National Personnel Record Center, St. Louis, MO.

36. Investigation Memorandum, March 14, 1919, in Alvin C. York, U.S. Army Service Record.

37. Extract from Cablegram, March 20, 1919, in Alvin C. York, U.S. Army Service Record.

38. Robert H. Ferrell, *In the Company of Generals: The World War I Diary of Pierpont L. Stackpole* (Columbia: University of Missouri, 2009), 160.

39. Ibid, 162.

40. Ibid, 163.

41. Ibid, 165.

42. Ibid, 164–165.

43. Henry Blaine Davis Jr, *Generals in Khaki* (Raleigh, NC: Pentland Press, 1998), 115, 231.

44. War Department, *Medal of Honor Citation*, General Orders No. 59, May 3, 1919, in Alvin C. York, U.S. Army Service Record, National Personnel Record Center, St. Louis, MO.

45. Cablegram from General Pershing, March 14, 1919, in Alvin C. York, U.S. Army Service Record, National Personnel Record Center, St. Louis, MO.

46. Joseph Cummings Chase, "Corporal York, General Pershing, and Others," *World's Work* 32 (April 1919), 636–653.

47. George Pattullo, "The Second Elder Gives Battle," *The Saturday Evening Post*, April 26, 1919, 3.

48. Theodore Peterson, *Magazines in the Twentieth Century* (Urbana: University of Illinois Press, 1964), 13.

49. "Historian Says York Correct," *Boston Herald*, October 2, 1929.

50. "Merrithew Declares He, Not York, Deserves Real Credit," *Boston Herald*, October 3, 1929.

51. Sandra Turner, *Sergeant Alvin C. York: The Making of a Hero and Legend*, (CreateSpace Independent Publishing Platform, 2015), 28.

52. "Roxbury Boy Challenges Sergt. York Legend," *The Sunday Republican*, Roxbury, CT, May 29, 1927.

53. "Unprecedented Honor to York," *Nashville Banner*, May 24, 1919.

54. "York to Visit Knoxville Again," *The Knoxville Sentinel*, May 29, 1919.

55. George Pattullo, "The Second Elder Gives Battle," Censor's Copy, AEF

General Headquarters G-2-D, Box 6162, Case 68–4, RG 120, Records of the American Expeditionary Forces, National Archives, Washington, DC, 1, 6.

56. Cablegram from General Pershing, March 14, 1919, in Alvin C. York, U.S. Army Service Record, National Personnel Record Center, St. Louis, MO.

57. Frank C. Phillips, "Signal Corps Photograph 49192," National Archives.

58. "Then and Now," *The American Legion Monthly*, Vol. 2, No. 5, May 1927, 57.

59. "Headquarters 164th Infantry Brigade," *General Orders No. 1*, May 4, 1919.

60. "Calls Sergt. York 'Bravest of Men,'" *The New York Times*, May 22, 1919.

61. "Sergt. York Here Proves Modest," *The Washington Times*, May 24, 1919.

62. "Says Sergt York Is Hero, But There Are Others," *Chattanooga Daily Times*, June 15, 1919.

63. Frank A. Holden, *War Memories* (Athens, GA: Athens Book Co., 1922), 13.

Chapter 4

1. "Sergt York Gets Great Reception," *The Boston Globe*, January 29, 1920.

2. "New Haven Sergeant May Share Honors of 'Greatest War Hero' with Alvin York," *Hartford Courant*, September 26, 1920.

3. "Colonel Buxton on the New America," *Norwich Bulletin*, February 21, 1920.

4. "New Haven Sergeant," *Hartford Courant*, September 26, 1920.

5. "Two Heroes Share Honor with York," *Hartford Courant*, September 23, 1929.

6. "Sergeant York Story Is Denied," *Providence Journal*, September 13, 1930.

7. Letter from Edward Buxton to George Duncan, April 22, 1932, George Brand Duncan Papers, 1882–1948, University of Kentucky Special Collections Research Center.

8. "New Haven Sergeant," *Hartford Courant*, September 26, 1920.

9. Letter from Edward Buxton to George Duncan, April 22, 1932.

10. "Alvin Cullum York has Clear Title," *The Albany-Decatur Daily*, May 29, 1922.

11. "York's Aide Made Member of Legion," *Boston Herald*, September 25, 1929.

12. "Then and Now," *The American Legion Monthly*, Vol. 2, No. 5, May 1927, 57.

13. Ibid.

14. "Roxbury Boy Challenges Sergt. York Legend," *The Sunday Republican*, Waterbury, CT, May 29, 1927.

15. "Man in York's Squad to go to Maneuvers," *The Boston Globe*, September 30, 1929.

16. *Military Exposition and Carnival Program* (Washington, DC: Army War College, 1929), 38.

17. David D. Lee, *Sergeant York: An American Hero* (Lexington: University Press of Kentucky, 1985), 39.

18. Letter from Henry Swindler to George Edward Buxton, July 17, 1929, records of the Army War College, Thomas File, RG 165.

19. Letter from E. C. B. Danforth to Henry Swindler, August 5, 1929, records of the Army War College, Thomas File, RG 165.

20. Douglas Mastriano, *Alvin York: A New Biography of the Hero of the Argonne*, (Lexington: University Press of Kentucky, 2014), 154.

21. *Military Exposition and Carnival Program*, 9.

22. "Back to War Again," *The St. Joseph News-Press,* October 1, 1929.

23. "Other Heroes with Sergt. York Are the True Forgotten Men," *Buffalo Evening News*, July 18, 1941.

24. "Can't Leave Cattle to Receive Hero's Honors," *The Springfield Sunday Union and Republican*, September 29, 1929.

25. "Sergt. York and Buddies to Be Feted," *Hartford Courant*, September 22, 1929.

26. Invitation from War Department to Otis B. Merrithew, September 16, 1929, Jimmy Fallon Collection. Italics in original.

27. "Attempt Made to Oust Alvin York," *The Daily News-Journal*, October 1, 1929.

28. "Says York Got Credit Due All," *The Boston Globe*, October 1, 1929.

29. Ibid.

30. "Merrithew Declares He, Not York, Deserves Real Credit," *Boston Herald*, October 3, 1929.

31. "Early and Beardsley to Fly to Washington," *Hartford Courant*, October 2, 1929.

32. "Sgt. York, "One-Man Army of Argonne, Replies to Attack on His Exploits," *The Tribune*, October 2, 1929.

33. "Army Officials Must be Shown," *Hartford Courant*, October 2, 1929.

34. "Chill Welcome for State Veteran Trio," *Hartford Courant*, October 3, 1929.

35. "War Heroes Agree to Avoid Clash on York Honors," *The New Haven Evening Register*, October 3, 1929.

36. "Chill Welcome for State Veteran Trio."

37. "Fall River Veteran Called Hidden Hero," *The Boston Globe*, October 2, 1929.

38. Saul Odess is an interesting character in the story of the Other Sixteen.

He claimed to be a member of the patrol. However, no evidence has ever been found to support his assertion. After the 1929 event, Odess invited Merrithew to a banquet and Merrithew supported the idea that Odess was originally part of the patrol. Why Merrithew supported him is unknown. No other men supported Odess, nor did Merrithew later, in 1941, consider him to be included. It can be proven that Odess was part of Company G, and perhaps he was assigned to accompany the men and the 132 prisoners after they left the woods.

39. "Claims Glory for Comrades," *The Boston Globe*, October 2, 1929.

40. "All of York Squad Will Be Given DSC," *The Boston Globe*, October 4, 1929.

41. Thomas Caren, "Men with York to Be Rewarded," *The Boston Herald*, October 4, 1929.

42. Bulkley S. Griffin, "York Squad Will Receive Decorations," *Hartford Courant*, October 4, 1929.

43. Letter from Otis Merrithew to His Wife, October 1929, Jimmy Fallon Collection.

44. Griffin, "York Squad Will Receive Decorations."

45. Caren, "Men with York to Be Rewarded."

46. "Secret Records Omit Mention of N. E. Heroes in Argonne Fray," *Boston Herald*, October 5, 1929.

47. "Law Prevents Medal Award to Member of York's Squad," *Boston Herald*, November 4, 1929.

48. "Secret Records Omit Mention of N. E. Heroes in Argonne Fray."

49. Griffin, "York Squad Awards May Be Delayed," *Hartford Courant*, October 5, 1919,

50. "York Platoon Commander to Be Decorated," *Journal Gazette*, October 5, 1929.

51. Ibid.

52. "Sergt Early Receives Belated Recognition," *The Boston Globe*, October 5, 1929.

53. Senator John A. Danaher, The Exploit of Bernard Early at Chatel-Chehery, *Congressional Record*, 77 (August 7, 1941): S 6864.

54. "City Plans Honor for Bernard Early," *The New Haven Evening Register*, October 6, 1929.

55. War Department, *General Orders No. 22*, December 31, 1929.

56. "City Plans Honor for Bernard Early," *The New Haven Evening Register*, October 6, 1929

57. "Return Home Gives Early Biggest Thrill," *New Haven Evening News*, October 7, 1929.

58. "City Plans Honor for Bernard Early," *New Haven Evening Register*, October 6, 1929.

59. "City Acclaims Sergt. Early DSC Wearer," *New Haven Evening Register*, October 12, 1929.

60. Ibid.

61. "Early Honored by New Haven," *Hartford Courant*, October 13, 1929.

62. "Sergt. York Invited to Early Fete," *New Haven Evening Register*, October 8, 1929.

63. "Early Honored by New Haven," *Hartford Courant*, October 13, 1929.

64. "Ovation Greets World War Hero," *New Haven Evening Register*, October 13, 1929.

65. "Sergt. Early is Awarded Hero's Medal," *Hartford Courant*, October 6, 1929.

66. Ibid.

67. Ibid.

68. Bulkley S. Griffin, "Down Washington Way," *Hartford Courant*, October 6, 1929.

69. Henry O. Swindler, "Turkey Match," *Infantry Journal* 37, no. 4 (October 1930), 343–351.

Chapter 5

1. "New Haven Sergeant May Share Honors of "Greatest War Hero" with Alvin York," *Hartford Courant*, September 26, 1920.

2. "Says York Got Credit Due All," *The Boston Globe*, October 1, 1929.

3. "War Heroes Agree to Avoid Clash on York Honors," *The New Haven Evening Register*, October 3, 1929.

4. "Konotski Leaves by Train Today for Washington," *Holyoke Daily Transcript*, October 2, 1929.

5. "Sergt. Early Is Awarded Medal," *Hartford Courant*, October 6, 1929.

6. Letter from Otis Merrithew to Senator David I. Walsh, October 15, 1929, Jimmy Fallon collection.

7. Letter from Leo Litz to John Connor, American Legion National Headquarters, November 13, 1929, Jimmy Fallon collection.

8. Robert Talley, "The Men Who Went Thru Hell with Sergt. York," *Public Opinion*, November 11, 1929.

9. "Brookline Man Aided York in Argonne Raid," *Arizona Republic*, February 9, 1930.

10. "Merrithew Case to Be Reopened," *The Boston Globe*, May 13, 1931.

11. House Bill, House of Representatives, *To allow the Distinguished Service cross for Service in the World War to be awarded to Otis B. Merrithew*, HR 7340, 71st Cong., 2nd sess., introduced in House December 11, 1929; HR 864, 72nd Cong., 1st sess., introduced in House December 8, 1931; HR 2427, 73rd Cong., 1st sess. introduced in House March 9, 1933.

12. "Files Bill to Confer DSC on Merrithew," *The Boston Globe*, December 11, 1929.

13. House Bill, House of Representatives, *To allow the Distinguished Service cross for Service in the World War to be awarded to Otis B. Merrithew.*

14. Letter from Otis Merrithew to Senator Marcus Coolidge, June 5, 1933, Jimmy Fallon collection.

15. Letter from Otis Merrithew to his Wife, 1929, Jimmy Fallon collection.

16. Letter from Edward Buxton to George Duncan, April 22, 1932, George Brand Duncan Papers, 1882–1948, University of Kentucky Special Collections Research Center.

17. Letter from G. E. Buxton to Otis Merrithew, October 8, 1929, Jimmy Fallon Collection.

18. "Law Prevents Medal Award to Member of York's Squad," *Boston Herald*, November 4, 1929.

19. Letter from G. E. Buxton to Otis Merrithew, October 8, 1929, Jimmy Fallon Collection.

20. Letter from G. E. Buxton to Otis Merrithew, October 28, 1929, Jimmy Fallon Collection; December 9, 1929, Jimmy Fallon Collection.

21. Sworn Statement of Otis Merrithew signed by Bernard Early, December 1, 1929; signed by Feodor Sok, October 31, 1929; signed by Patrick Donohue, October 31, 1929; signed by Percy Beardsley, November 15, 1929.

22. Letter from G. E. Buxton to Otis Merrithew, October 8, 1929, Jimmy Fallon Collection.

23. Letter from G. E. Buxton to Otis Merrithew, February 21, 1930, Jimmy Fallon Collection.

24. Letter from G. E. Buxton to Otis Merrithew, April 2, 1930, Jimmy Fallon Collection

25. Letter from G. E. Buxton to Otis Merrithew, April 16, 1930, Jimmy Fallon Collection.

26. Letter from Julian R. Lindsey to The Adjutant General, April 18, 1930, Jimmy Fallon Collection.

27. "Sergeant York Story Is Denied," *Providence Journal*, September 13, 1930.

28. Ibid.

29. Letter from G. E. Buxton to Otis Merrithew, May 19, 1931, Jimmy Fallon Collection.

30. Letter from G. E. Buxton to Otis Merrithew, May 29, 1931, Jimmy Fallon Collection.

31. Letter from G. E. Buxton to Otis Merrithew, June 11, 1931, Jimmy Fallon Collection.

32. Letter from G. E. Buxton to Otis Merrithew, June 27, 1931, Jimmy Fallon Collection.

33. Letter from Bertha Hartley to Otis Merrithew, March 3, 1932, Jimmy Fallon Collection.

34. Letter from Edward Buxton to George Duncan, April 22, 1932, George Brand Duncan Papers, 1882–1948, University of Kentucky Special Collections Research Center.

35. "Purple Heart," War Department, June 27, 1932, Jimmy Fallon Collection.

36. Letter from G. E. Buxton to Otis Merrithew, October 24, 1932, Jimmy Fallon Collection.

37. Letter from Bertha Hartley to Otis Merrithew, December 29, 1932, Jimmy Fallon Collection.

38. Letter from James McKinley to Otis Merrithew, November 22, 1933, Jimmy Fallon Collection.

39. Letter from Feodor Sok to Edward C. B. Danforth, May 16, 1933, Jimmy Fallon Collection.

40. "Other Heroes with Sergt. York Are the True Forgotten Men," *Buffalo Evening News*, July 18, 1941.

41. Letter from William Payton to Otis Merrithew, April 2, 1933, Jimmy Fallon Collection.

42. Letter from Otis Merrithew to Senator Marcus Coolidge, April 24, 1935, Jimmy Fallon Collection.

43. Letter from Senator Marcus Coolidge to Otis Merrithew, June 22, 1935, Jimmy Fallon Collection.

44. "Medal of Honor for Bernard Early Resolution," American Legion Department of Connecticut, August 10, 1935.

45. "Connecticut Legion Post Says York Did Not Capture Huns," *Corsicana Daily Sun*, August 10, 1935.

46. "Claim Hero Given False War Credit," *The Californian*, August 10, 1935.

47. "Legion Asks That Hero be Honored," *Hartford Courant*, August 11, 1935.

48. "York's Commander Scoffs at Claims," *The Courier-Journal*, August 12, 1935.

49. "Georgia Buddy Supports Early," *Hartford Courant*, August 22, 1935.

50. House Bill, House of Representatives, *Authorizing the President of the United States to appoint Corp. Bernard Early as a major in the United States Army and then place him on the retired list*, HR 8420, 75th Cong., 2nd sess., introduced in House November 17, 1937.

51. Barron C. Watson, "The Men Who Helped a Hero," *Ken*, April 21, 1938, 87.

52. Ibid., 89.

Chapter 6

1. Michael Birdwell, *Celluloid Soldiers: Warner Bros.'s Campaign against Nazism* (New York: New York University Press, 2001), 1.

2. "Film Money-Makers Selected by Variety," *The New York Times*, December 31, 1941.

3. 1942 Oscars, *www.oscars.org/oscars/ceremonies/1942*.

4. The 100 Most Inspiring Films of All Time, American Film Institute, *www.afi.com/afis-100-years-100-cheers*.

5. National Film Registry, Library of Congress, *www.loc.gov/programs/national-film-preservation-board/film-registry/complete-national-film-registry-listing*.

6. Thomas Doherty, *Projections of War: Hollywood, American Culture, and World War II* (New York: Columbia University Press, 1993), 100.

7. Birdwell, *Celluloid Soldiers*, 2, 101.

8. Ibid., 102.

9. Ibid., 108.

10. Letter from John S. Hale to Walter Bruington, June 3, 1940, *Sergeant York* Files, Box A-52, Folder 2880, Warner Bros. Archives.

11. Letter from Otis Merrithew to Jesse Lasky, June 12, 1940, *Sergeant York* Files, Box A-52, Folder 2880, Warner Bros. Archives.

12. "Inter-Office Communication," *Sergeant York* Files, Box A-52, Folder 2880, Warner Bros. Archives.

13. Letter from John Hale to Walter Bruington, June 3, 1940.

14. Ibid.

15. Letter from Roy Obringer to Jacob Wilk, *Sergeant York* Files, Box A-52, Folder 2880, Warner Bros. Archives.

16. Birdwell, *Celluloid Soldiers*, 209.

17. Letter from Bill Guthrie to Otis Merrithew, October 29, 1940, Jimmy Fallon Collection.

18. "Re: Sergeant York," October 21, 1940, *Sergeant York* Files, Box A-52, Folder 2880, Warner Bros. Archives.

19. "Otis Merrithew Contract," *Sergeant York* Files, Box A-52, Folder 2880, Warner Bros. Archives.

20. Frederick C. Othman, "Heroism Pays Dividends," *Seminole Producer*, January 10, 1941.

21. "Inter-Office Communication," April 4, 1941, *Sergeant York* Files, Box A-52, Folder 2880, Warner Bros. Archives.

22. "Inter-Office Communication," April 16, 1941, *Sergeant York* Files, Box A-52, Folder 2880, Warner Bros. Archives.

23. Letter from Bill Guthrie to Otis Merrithew, November 25, 1940, Jimmy Fallon Collection.

24. Letter from Otis Merrithew to Bill Guthrie, Undated, Jimmy Fallon Collection.

25. Letter from Otis Merrithew to Bill Guthrie, Undated, Jimmy Fallon Collection.

26. Letter from Bill Guthrie to Otis Merrithew, December 10, 1940, Jimmy Fallon Collection.

27. "Inter-Office Communication," April 4, 1941, *Sergeant York* Files.

28. Letter from Bill Guthrie to Otis Merrithew, December 10, 1940, Jimmy Fallon Collection.

29. Letter from Bill Guthrie to Otis Merrithew, December 26, 1940, Jimmy Fallon Collection.

30. "Dear Mr. Perkins," April 26, 1941, *Sergeant York* Files, Box A-52, Folder 2880, Warner Bros. Archives.

31. Letter from Bill Guthrie to Otis Merrithew, December 26, 1940, Jimmy Fallon Collection.

32. Letter from Joseph Kornacki to Otis Merrithew, January 18, 1941, Jimmy Fallon Collection.

33. Frederick C. Othman, "Recognition Will Go to Sgt. York's Squad in Movie," *Hattiesburg American*, January 9, 1941.

34. Frederick C. Othman, "Scout Digs Up York's Buddies," *The Coos Bay Times*, January 10, 1918; Frederick C. Othman, "Heroism Pays Dividends to Farmer, Bum, Truck Driver, Dump Dweller, and Waiter," *Seminole Producer*, January 10, 1941.

35. To illustrate how the other survivors were portrayed in the media, I have made a random selection of six newspapers from around the country that published the article written by Othman. These are the *Seminole Producer* of Seminole, Oklahoma; *The Boston Globe* of Boston; *The Coos Bay Times* of Marshfield, Oregon; *The Daily Chronicle* of De Kalb, Illinois; and *The Ogden Standard* of Ogden, Utah.

36. Frederick C. Othman, "Heroism Pays Dividends," *Seminole Producer*, January 10, 1941.

37. Frederick C. Othman, "Sergt. York's Heroic Detail Finally Receives Cash Award," *The Boston Globe*, January 10, 1941.

38. Frederick C. Othman, "Hollywood Scout Scours Country," *The Coos Bay Times*, January 10, 1941.

39. Frederick C. Othman, "World War Heroes Get Cash Dividends Today," *The Daily Chronicle*, January 10, 1941.

40. "Scout Digs Up York's Buddies," *The Coos Bay Times*, January 10, 1941.

41. "Argonne Heroes Movie Acclaims York Comrades," *The Ogden Standard-Examiner*, January 10, 1940.

42. "Hero of Argonne Sells Name to Films," *The Philadelphia Inquirer*, January 11, 1941.

43. "Unsung Denison War Hero Lives in Quiet Obscurity," *The Whitewright Sun*, January 16, 1941.

44. Letter from Bill Guthrie to Otis Merrithew, January 17, 1941, Jimmy Fallon Collection.

45. Letter from Otis Merrithew to Bill Guthrie, March 11, 1941, *Sergeant York* Files, Box A-52, Folder 2880, Warner Bros. Archives.

46. Abem Finkle, "The Sad Story of Sgt. York," *Sergeant York* Files, Box A-52, Warner Bros. Archives. Quoted in Birdwell, *Celluloid Soldiers,* 123.

47. Letter from Bill Guthrie to Otis Merrithew, March 18, 1941, Jimmy Fallon Collection.

48. Ibid.

49. Letter from Joseph Kornacki to Otis Merrithew, March 27, 1941, Jimmy Fallon Collection.

50. "Inter-Office Communication," April 10, 1941, *Sergeant York* Files, Box A-52, Folder 2880, Warner Bros. Archives.

51. "Inter-Office Communication," April 16, 1941, *Sergeant York* Files, Box A-52, Folder 2880, Warner Bros. Archives.

52. Letter from Roy Obringer to R. W. Perkins, April 26, 1941, *Sergeant York* Files, Box A-52, Folder 2880, Warner Bros. Archives.

53. Ibid.

54. Ibid.

55. Letter from Bill Guthrie to Otis Merrithew, May 9, 1941, Jimmy Fallon Collection.

56. Letter from Roy Obringer to R. W. Perkins, May 10, 1941, *Sergeant York* Files, Box A-52, Folder 2880, Warner Bros. Archives.

57. Ibid.

58. Letter from Joseph Kornacki to Otis Merrithew, May 21, 1941, Jimmy Fallon Collection.

59. Letter from Otis Merrithew to Jesse Lasky, June 29, 1941, Jimmy Fallon Collection.

60. Paul Harrison, "Screen Chats," *Shamokin News-Dispatch*, July 30, 1941.

61. John Chapman, "Looking at Hollywood," *Chicago Tribune*, July 2, 1941.

62. Harrison, "Screen Chats."

63. John Chapman, "Hollywood," *Daily News*, July 6, 1941.

64. Harrison, "Screen Chats," *Shamokin News-Dispatch*, July 30, 1941.

65. Chapman, "Hollywood."

66. Ibid.

67. Harrison, "Screen Chats."

68. Chapman, "Hollywood."

69. Ibid.

70. Kate Joyce, "Letter to the Legionnaires," *Albany Times-Union*, July 20, 1941.

71. Ibid.

72. Harrison, "Screen Chats."

73. Ibid.

74. Transcript of *We the People*, July 1, 1941, Alvin C. York Papers. Quoted in Birdwell, *Celluloid Soldiers*, 112–113.

75. Birdwell, *Celluloid Soldiers*, 125.

76. Clayton Koppes and Gregory Black, *Hollywood Goes to War: How Politics, Profits, and Propaganda Shaped World War II Movies* (Berkeley: University of California Press, 1990), 39.

77. "Roosevelt Tells Sergt. Alvin York Movie Thrilled Him," *St. Louis Post-Dispatch*, July 30, 1941.

78. Birdwell, *Celluloid Soldiers*, 120.

79. George Pattullo, "The Second Elder Gives Battle," *The Saturday Evening Post*, April 26, 1919, 73.

80. Samuel K. Cowan, *Sergeant York and His People* (New York: Funk and Wagnalls, 1922), 12–13.

81. "Sergeant York to Benefit Bible School of Hero," *New York Herald Tribune*, July 3, 1941.

82. Birdwell, *Celluloid Soldiers*, 122.

83. Harry Parsons File, *Sergeant York* Files, Box A-52, Warner Bros. Archives. Quoted in Birdwell, *Celluloid Soldiers*, 114.

84. Letter from Otis Merrithew to Bernard Early, July 14, 1941, Jimmy Fallon Collection.

85. Letter from Otis Merrithew et al. to the Editor of the *Boston Globe*, July 14, 1941, Jimmy Fallon Collection.

86. Letter from Bill Guthrie to Otis Merrithew, July 25, 1941, Jimmy Fallon Collection.

87. Jesse L. Lasky, *I Blow My Own Horn* (Garden City, NY: Doubleday Company, 1957), 259.

88. Senator Kenneth D. McKellar, Promotion of Alvin C. York to the Rank of Colonel, *Congressional Record*, 77 (July 29, 1941): S 6411.

89. Senator John A. Danaher, The exploit of Bernard Early at Chatel-Chehery, *Congressional Record*, 77 (August 7, 1941): S 6864.

90. Senator Alexander Wiley, Promotion of Alvin C. York to the Rank of Colonel, *Congressional Record*, 77 (July 29, 1941): S 6413.

Chapter 7

1. Michael Birdwell, *Celluloid Soldiers: Warner Bros.'s Campaign against Nazism* (New York: New York University Press, 2001), 129.

2. *Propaganda in Motion Pictures: Hearings before a Senate Subcommittee on Interstate Commerce*, United States Senate, 87th Cong., 2nd sess. (Washington, DC: Government Printing Office, 1942), 346.

3. Birdwell, *Celluloid Soldiers*, 171.

4. "Sgt. York Phony Hero," *Sunday Herald*, January 4, 1942.

5. Ibid.

6. Letter from Mrs. George S. Barnes, August 14, 1941, in Alvin C. York, U.S. Army Service Record, National Personnel Record Center, St. Louis, MO.

7. "Receives Silver Star for Part He Played in Assisting Sergeant York Accomplish Heroic Feat," *The Evening Tribune*, February 21, 1945.

8. Letter from Jeanne Merrithew to Senator Edward Kennedy, February 4, 1963, Edward M. Kennedy Senate Files, Box 514, "1962–1964: F-5 Merrithew, Otis B," JFK Library.

9. Letter from Senator Edward Kennedy to Jeanne Merrithew, February 9, 1963.

10. Letter from Harry Ritchey to Senator Edward Kennedy, February 25, 1963.

11. Letter from Jeanne Merrithew Faye to Senator Edward Kennedy, March 6, 1963.

12. Letter from Otis B. Merrithew to Senator Edward Kennedy, September 9, 1964, Edward M. Kennedy Senate Files, box 355, "1962–1964: F-4 Merrithew, Otis B," JFK Library.

13. Letter from Brigadier General L. H. Walker Jr to Senator Edward Kennedy, September 24, 1964.

14. Letter from Otis Merrithew to Senator Edward Kennedy, October 4, 1964.

15. Letter from Otis Merrithew to Senator Edward Kennedy, February 8, 1965.

16. Letter from Otis Merrithew to Senator Edward Kennedy, June 18, 1965.

17. Letter from Otis Merrithew to President Lyndon B. Johnson, "Cutti," Box 562, Name File C, White House Central File, LBJ Library.

18. Letter from Lieutenant General J. K. Woolnough to Otis Merrithew, September 8, 1965, Jimmy Fallon Collection.

19. Letter from Lieutenant General J. K. Woolnough to Otis Merrithew, September 13, 1965, Jimmy Fallon Collection.

20. "For Role with Sgt. York World War I Veteran to Get Silver Star," *The Courier-Journal*, September 20, 1965.

21. Letter from Henry Lieberman to Otis Merrithew, September 27, 1965, Jimmy Fallon Collection.

22. Letter from the Board of Selectman to Otis Merrithew, October 4, 1965, Jimmy Fallon Collection.

23. Otis Merrithew Silver Star Certificate, Office of the Adjutant General, U.S. Army, Jimmy Fallon Collection.

24. "Silver Star Awarded Chestnut Hill World War I Veteran Official Release," "Merrimana," Box 375, Name File M, White House Central File, LBJ Library.

25. Letter from Otis Merrithew to President Lyndon Johnson, "Merrimana," Box 375, Name File M, White House Central File, LBJ Library.

26. Letter from Major General J. C. Lambert to Otis Merrithew, December 7, 1965, Jimmy Fallon Collection.

27. Letter from Percy Beardsley to Otis Merrithew, January 3, 1966, Jimmy Fallon Collection.

28. "Brookline Veteran Recalls Argonne," *The Boston Globe,* October 8, 1968.

29. *Marriage Records. Pennsylvania Marriages.* Various County Register of Wills Offices, Pennsylvania.

30. *1930*; Census Place: *Ashley, Luzerne, Pennsylvania*; Page: *5B*; Enumeration District: *0003*; FHL microfilm: *2341800*.

31. "Sergt. York's Buddy Here Got $20, Not $250, For Use of His Name," *Buffalo Evening News,* March 3, 1941.

32. "Denison Rites Set for York's Buddy," *Fort Worth Star-Telegram,* September 26, 1961.

33. Representative Thomas J. Lane, In Memory of "Paddy" Donohue—a Member of Sergeant York's Famous Squad in World War I, *Congressional Record,* 87 (February 19, 1962): S 2501.

34. Keith Eddings, "Gallantry in Action," *Eagle Tribune,* April 18, 2016.

35. "Brookline War Hero Stops Runaway Car," *Boston Herald,* July 3, 1930.

36. Interview with Jimmy Fallon, December 27, 2019.

37. "Merrithew Square Stands in Patriotic Tribute to Man Who was Once Overlooked," *The Brookline Chronicle,* October 13, 1977.

38. U.S. Congress, *Public Law 104–106 (National Defense Authorization Act),* S 1124, 104th Cong., February 10, 1996, 129–130.

39. "Someone Helped," *The Evening Sun,* September 23, 1965.

Chapter 8

1. Laurence Stallings, *The Doughboys: The Story of the AEF, 1917–1918* (New York: Harper & Row, 1963), 297–301.

2. Robert Ellis Cahill, *New England's Little Known War Wonders* (Peabody, MA: Chandler-Smith Publishing, 1984), 30–39.

3. "Silver Star Awarded Chestnut Hill World War I Veteran Press Release," "Merrimana," Box 375, Name File M, White House Central File, Lyndon B. Johnson Library.

4. David D. Lee, *Sergeant York: An American Hero* (Lexington: University Press of Kentucky, 1985), 36, 107.

5. John Perry, *Sgt. York: His Life, Legacy, and Legend* (Nashville, TN: Broadman & Holman, 1997), 9, 85, 112, 214, 248, 257.

6. Michael Birdwell, *Celluloid Soldiers: Warner Bros.'s Campaign against Nazism* (New York: New York University Press, 2001), 113–114.

7. "The Sergeant and Miss Gracie," *Sgt. York Says: Official Publication of the Sgt. York Patriotic Foundation,* Vol. 1, No. 2 (Spring-Summer 2000), 4.

8. Edward G. Lengel, *To Conquer Hell: The Meuse-Argonne, 1918, The Epic Battle That Ended the First World War* (New York: Henry Holt, 2008), 279–282.

9. Douglas Mastriano, *Sergeant York Discovery Expedition (SYDE) Report on the Discovery of Where Alvin C. York Earned the Medal of Honor 08 October 1918,* January 2007, *www.sgtyorkdiscorvery.com*, 37; Thomas J. Nolan, "Battlefield Landscapes: Geographic Information Science as a Method of Integrating History and Archeology for Battlefield Interpretation" (Texas State University at San Marcos, Department of Geography, 2007).

10. Douglas Mastriano, *Alvin York: A New Biography of the Hero of the Argonne* (Lexington: University Press of Kentucky, 2014), 1, 3, 109, 153, 171.

11. Ibid., 155.

12. American Battle Monuments Commission, *World War I Battlefield Companion,* (Washington, DC: Government Printing Office, 2018)

13. Laura A. Macaluso, *New Haven in World War I* (Charleston, SC: History Press, 2017).

14. Michael Kelly, *Hero on the Western Front: Discovering Alvin York's WWI Battlefield* (Philadelphia: Frontline Books, 2018), 288, 301–322.

15. Richard S. Faulkner, *Meuse Argonne: 26 September-11 November 1918* (Washington, DC: Center of Military History, 2018), 36–38.

16. Association of the United States Army, *Medal of Honor: Alvin York* (2018), *www.ausa.org/york*.

17. James Carl Nelson, *The York Patrol: The Real Story of Alvin York and the Unsung Heroes Who Made Him World War I's Most Famous Soldier* (New York: William Morrow, 2021), 107.

18. Ibid., 112.

19. Ibid., 115.

20. Ibid., 161, 116.

21. Ibid., 183.

22. Ibid., 221, 241.

23. Ibid., 221.

24. Ibid., 231.

Chapter 9

1. Scott Chandler, *History of the Three Hundred and Twenty-Eighth Regiment of Infantry, Eighty-Second Division* (Atlanta: Foote and Davies, 1920), 43.

2. Burial File of 2nd Lt. Kirby Stewart, Box 4700, RG 92, Records of the Graves Registration Services, NARA College Park, MD

3. *History of the Three Hundred and Twenty-Eighth Infantry*, 45.

4. Michael Kelly, *Hero on the Western Front: Discovering Alvin York's WWI Battlefield* (Philadelphia: Frontline Books, 2018), 24.

5. "War Hero Eager to See Himself Portrayed in Movie of Exploit," *The Evening Tribune*, November 29, 1941.

6. "New Haven Sergeant May Share Honors of 'Greatest War Hero' with Alvin York," *The Hartford Daily Courant,* September 26, 1920.

7. "2. Landwehr Division Kriegtagebuch und Anlagen 1.10.18—10.10.18," *2nd Landwehr Division War Diary and Annexes 1 October, 1918—10 October, 1918,* (College Park, MD: National Archives and Records Administration), Record Group 165, Folder II, 864—33.5. Translated by Brad Posey.

8. "Testimony of German Officers and Men about Sergeant York," translated by the US Army War College, Carlisle, PA, June, 1936, 14; Some of this information had been published in the Summer 2020 edition of *Infantry Magazine* in my article "Forgotten Soldiers: The Other Sixteen at Chatel-Chéhéry." However, new information came to light after its publication. Therefore, this book contains the correct designations of the German units.

9. Statement of Otis B. Merrithew sworn to by Patrick J. Donohue, October 31, 1929, Jimmy Fallon Collection. Thomas J. Nolan, "Geographic Information Science as a Method of Integrating History and Archeology for Battlefield Interpretation," *Journal of Conflict Archeology*, Vol. 5 (2009), 95.

10. Statement of Otis B. Merrithew sworn to by Patrick J. Donohue, October 31, 1919; "New Haven Sergeant May Share Honors of 'Greatest War Hero' with Alvin York," *The Hartford Daily Courant,* September 26, 1920.

11. "New Haven Sergeant May Share Honors of "Greatest War Hero" with Alvin York."

12. Testimony of German Officers and Men about Sergeant York," 5–7; G. Edward Buxton Jr, *Official History of the 82nd Division, AEF, 1917–1919,* 60–61.

13. "Testimony of German Officers and Men about Sergeant York," 19–20; "Manner in Which Murray Savage Died," *Ontario County Journal*, February 7, 1919.

14. "New Haven Sergeant May Share Honors of 'Greatest War Hero' with Alvin York," *Hartford Courant*, September 26, 1920.

15. Eye-witness statement by Pvt. Michael Sacina, Burial File of Corporal Murray Savage, Box 4297, RG 92, Records of the Graves Registration Services, NARA College Park, MD.

16. Eye-witness statement by Pvt. Michael Sacina, Burial File of Private

Maryan Dymowski, Box 1455, RG 92, Records of the Graves Registration Services, NARA College Park, MD.

17. Eye-witness statement by Pvt. Michael Sacina, Burial File of Private Carl Swanson, Box 4781, RG 92, Records of the Graves Registration Services, NARA College Park, MD.

18. Burial File of Private Fred Wareing, Box 5092; Burial File of Private Ralph Weiler, Box 5141; Burial File of William Wine, Box 5286, RG 92, Records of the Graves Registration Services, NARA College Park, MD.

19. Thomas J. Nolan GIS Records mapped by University of Oklahoma geography student Arturo Garcia.

20. Letter from Edward Buxton to George Duncan, April 22, 1932, George Brand Duncan Papers, 1882–1948, University of Kentucky Special Collections Research Center. Thomas J. Nolan, "Geographic Information Science as a Method of Integrating History and Archeology for Battlefield Interpretation," *Journal of Conflict Archeology*, Vol. 5 (2009), 95.

21. "Says York Got Credit Due All," *The Boston Globe*, October 1, 1929.

22. "Percy Beardsley's Claims to Honor," *Hartford Courant*, May 29, 1927.

23. Statement of Michael Sacina taken by G. Edward Buxton, printed in Alvin C. York, *Sergeant York: His Own Life Story and War Diary*, edited by Tom Skeyhill (Garden City, NY: Doubleday, Doran, 1928), 253.

24. "Others Who Fought Beside Sergeant York," *The Boston Sunday Globe*, May 29, 1927.

25. "Boys Who Fought Beside Sergeant York Share Famous Spotlight That Shines on "One-Man-Army," *Boston Sunday Post*, May 29, 1927.

26. "Percy Beardsley's Claim to Honors," *Hartford Courant*, May 29, 1927. Thomas J. Nolan, "Geographic Information Science as a Method of Integrating History and Archeology for Battlefield Interpretation," *Journal of Conflict Archeology*, Vol. 5 (2009), 96.

27. "Boys Who Fought Beside Sergeant York Share Famous Spotlight That Shines on "One-Man-Army"; "Percy Beardsley's Claim to Honors."

28. G. Edward Buxton Jr., *Official History of the 82nd Division, AEF, 1917–1919* (Indianapolis, IN: Bobbs-Merrill, 1919), 61; This is the basis of the "turkey shoot" and bayonet charge myth. However, neither is mentioned in the original statements. Douglass Mastriano claimed the man shot was Lt. Fritz Endriss, but the German accounts do not place him in the initial fight.

29. Affidavit of Michael Sacina, January 26, 1919, found in York, *Sergeant York*, 253.

30. Capt. Frank E. Pike, "Clinical Record Brief," Evacuation Hospital 28, October 16, 1918; Letter from Edward Buxton to George Duncan, April 22, 1932, George Brand Duncan Papers, 1882–1948, University of Kentucky Special Collections Research Center.

31. "Percy Beardsley's Claim to Honors," *Hartford Courant*, May 29, 1927.

32. "Says York Got Credit Due All," *The Boston Globe*, October 1, 1929.

33. "Personal Akten von Lt. Thoma, Personal Records of Lieutenant Thoma" (München: Bayerische Hauptstaatsarchiv, Abteilung IV Kriegsarchiv), OP 14800. Translated by Brad Posey.

34. "War Hero Eager to See Himself Portrayed in Movie of Exploit," *The Evening Tribune*, November 29, 1941; "Shares War Glory of Fighting Elder," *Evening Public Ledger*, May 24, 1919.

35. "Guilford Boy Reveals Real Inside Story of Sergt. York's Heroism," *Hartford Courant*, February 23, 1920; Letter from Edward Buxton to George Duncan, April 22, 1932, George Brand Duncan Papers, 1882–1948, University of Kentucky Special Collections Research Center.

36. "Georgia Buddy Says Sergeant Early Hero of Argonne Forest Engagement," *Hartford Courant*, August 22, 1935.

37. Letter from Edward Buxton to George Duncan, April 22, 1932, George Brand Duncan Papers, 1882–1948, University of Kentucky Special Collections Research Center.

38. Sworn Affidavit of 1st Lt Joseph A. Woods, in Alvin C. York, U.S. Army Service Record, National Personnel Record Center, St. Louis, MO.

39. "Merrithew Says He was Leader," *The Boston Globe*, October 3, 1929; "War Hero Eager to See Himself Portrayed in Movie of Exploit," *The Evening Tribune*, November 29, 1941.

40. "Shares War Glory of Fighting Elder," *Evening Public Ledger*, May 24, 1919; Alvin C. York, *Sergeant York: His Own Life Story and War Diary*, edited by Tom Skeyhill (Garden City, NY: Doubleday, Doran, 1928), 235.

Epilogue

1. "Roxbury Boy Challenges Sergt. York Legend," *The Sunday Republican*, Waterbury, CT, May 29, 1927.

2. Ibid.

3. Ibid.

Bibliography

Articles

Bellah, Robert. "Civil Religion in America." *Daedalus* 96, no. 1 (Winter 1967): 1–21.

Beattie, Taylor V. "In Search of York: Man, Myth and Legend." *Army History*, No. 50 (Summer-Fall 2000): 1–14.

Beattie, Taylor V. "Continuing the Search for York." *Army History*, No. 66 (Winter 2008): 20–28.

Chase, Joseph Cummings. "Corporal York, General Pershing, and Others." *World's Work* 37 (April 1919): 636–653.

Legg, James B. "Research: Finding Sergeant York." *Legacy*, Vol. 14, No. 1 (February 2010): 18–22.

Mahoney, Tom. "Alvin York and Frank Luke: Legendary WWI Heroes." *The American Legion Magazine* (November 1968): 22, 45–49.

McGinty, Brian. "Alvin York: Soldier of the Lord." *American History Illustrated* (November 1986): 40–41.

Meulebrouck, Stephan van. "Hot on the York Trail?" *The Western Front Association* No. 84 (June/July 2009): 27–31.

Nolan, Thomas J. "Geographic Information Science as a Method of Integrating History and Archeology for Battlefield Interpretation." *Journal of Conflict Archeology*, Vol. 5 (2009): 81–104.

Pattullo, George. "The Second Elder Gives Battle." *The Saturday Evening Post* (April 26, 1919): 3–4, 71–74.

Posey, Brad. "Re-Fighting the Meuse-Argonne: Alvin York and the Battle over World War I Site Commemoration." *Tennessee Historical Quarterly* Vol. 72, No. 4 (Winter 2012): 276–293.

"Sgt. Alvin York." *Newsweek* (November 11, 2019): 38–39.

Swindler, Henry O. "Turkey Match." *Infantry Journal* 37, no. 4 (October 1930), 343–351.

"Then and Now." *The American Legion Monthly*, Vol. 2, No. 5 (May 1927): 57.

Watson, Barron C. "The Men Who Helped a Hero." *Ken* (April 21, 1938): 87–89.

York, Alvin C. "The Diary of Sergeant York." *Liberty Magazine* (July 14, 1928): 7–10.

Books

American Battle Monuments Commission. *American Armies and Battlefields in Europe*. Washington, DC: Government Printing Office, 1938.

American Battle Monuments Commission. *World War I Battlefield Companion*. Washington, DC: Government Printing Office, 2018.

Association of the United States Army. *Medal of Honor: Alvin York*. 2018. *www.ausa.org/york*.

Birdwell, Michael. *Celluloid Soldiers: Warner Bros.'s Campaign against Nazism*. New York: New York University Press, 2001.

Brownrigg, Jeff. *Anzac Cove to Hollywood: The Story of Tom Skeyhill, Master of Deception*. Spit Junction, NSW: Anchor Books Australia, 2010.

Buxton, G. Edward. *Official History of the 82nd Division, AEF, 1917–1919*. Indianapolis, IN Bobbs-Merrill, 1919.

Cahill, Robert Ellis. *New England's Little Known War Wonders*. Peabody, MA: Chandler-Smith Publishing, 1984.

Chandler, Scott. *History of the Three Hundred and Twenty-Eighth Regiment of Infantry, Eighty-Second Division*. Atlanta: Foote and Davies, 1920.

Cowan, Samuel K. *Sergeant York and His People*. New York: Funk and Wagnalls, 1922.

Davis, Henry Blaine, Jr. *Generals in Khaki*. Raleigh, NC: Pentland Press, 1998.

Desfosses, Yves, Alain Jacques, and Gilles Prilaux. *Great War Archaeology*. Ouest, France, May 7, 2009.

Doherty, Thomas. *Projections of War: Hollywood, American Culture, and World War II*. New York: Columbia University Press, 1993.

Drury, David. *Hartford in World War I*. Charleston, SC: The History Press, 2015.

Faulkner, Richard S. *Meuse Argonne: 26 September–11 November 1918*. Washington, DC: Center of Military History, 2018.

Fitzpatrick, Kevin C. *World War I New York: A Guide to the City's Enduring Ties to the Great War*. Guilford, CT: Globe Pequot, 2017.

Hall, Clifford J., and John P. Lehn. *York County and the World War: 1914–1919*. Self-published, 1920.

Haulsee, W.M., F. G. Howe, and A. C. Doyle. *Soldiers of the Great War*. Washington, DC: Soldiers Record Publishing Association, 1920.

Herder, Brian Lane. *The Meuse-Argonne Offensive 1918*. Oxford: Osprey Publishing, 2020.

Holden, Frank A. *War Memories*. Athens, GA: Athens Book Co., 1922.

Humble, R. G. *Sgt. Alvin C. York : A Christian Patriot*. Circleville, OH: Advocate Publishing House, 1966.

Isenberg, Michael T. *War on Film: the American Cinema and World War I, 1914–1941*. Rutherford, NJ: Fairleigh Dickinson University Press, 1981.

Kelly, Michael. *Sergeant York of the Argonne Tour Guide*. Ennogra Forest Publication, 2008.

Kelly, Michael. *Hero on the Western Front: Discovering Alvin York's WWI Battlefield*. Philadelphia: Frontline Books, 2018.

Koppes, Clayton, and Gregory Black. *Hollywood Goes to War: How Politics, Profits, and Propaganda Shaped World War II Movies*. Berkeley: University of California Press, 1990.

Lasky, Jesse L. *I Blow My Own Horn*. Garden City, NY: Doubleday, 1957.

Lee, David D. *Sergeant York: An American Hero*. Lexington: University Press of Kentucky, 1985.

Lengel, Edward G. *To Conquer Hell: The Meuse-Argonne, 1918, The Epic Battle That Ended the First World War*. New York: Henry Holt, 2008.

Licursi, Kimberly J. Lamay. *Remembering World War I in America*. Lincoln: University of Nebraska Press, 2018.

Macaluso, Laura A. *New Haven in World War I*. Charleston, SC: The History Press, 2017.

Mastriano, Douglas. *Alvin York: A New Biography of the Hero of the Argonne*. Lexington: University Press of Kentucky, 2014.

Men of America: Sgt. Alvin C. York. Chicago: Stevens-Davis Co., 1929.

Military Exposition and Carnival Program. Washington, DC: U.S. Army War College, 1929.

Nolan, Thomas J. "Battlefield Landscapes: Geographic Information Science as a Method of Integrating History and Archeology for Battlefield Interpretation." Texas State University at San Marcos, Department of Geography, 2007.

Perry, John. *Sgt. York: His Life, Legacy, & Legend*. Nashville, TN: Broadman & Holman, 1997.

Peterson, Theodore. *Magazines in the Twentieth Century*. Urbana: University of Illinois Press, 1964.

Robertson, Breanne. *Investigating Iwo: The Flag Raisings in Myth, Memory, & Esprit de Corps*. Quantico, VA: Marine Corps History Division, 2019.

Schoner, Scott R. *82d Division, A.E.F., Unit Reports on the Meuse-Argonne Offensive*. The Doughboy Memorial Press, 2020.

Seldes, George. *Tell the Truth and Run*. New York: Greenburg, 1953.

Sgt. York Says: Official Publication of the Sgt. York Patriotic Foundation. Vol. 1, No. 1, Winter 2000.

Sgt. York Says: Official Publication of the Sgt. York Patriotic Foundation. Vol. 1, No. 2, Spring-Summer 2000.

Sgt. York Says: Official Publication of the Sgt. York Patriotic Foundation. Vol. 2, No. 1, Spring 2001.

Sgt. York Says: Official Publication of the Sgt. York Patriotic Foundation. Issue Number Five, October, 2001.

Sgt. York Says: Official Publication of the Sgt. York Patriotic Foundation. Vol. 3, No. 1, 2002.

Sgt. York Says: Official Publication of the Sgt. York Patriotic Foundation. Vol. 3, No. 2, 2002.

Sgt. York Says: Official Publication of the Sgt. York Patriotic Foundation. Vol. 4, No. 1, 2003.

Sgt. York Says: Official Publication of the Sgt. York Patriotic Foundation. Vol. 4, No. 2, 2003.

Skeyhill, Tom. *Sergeant York: Last of the Long Hunters.* Philadelphia: Winston, 1930.

Smith, Hutledge. *World War Record of Ex-Soldiers of Fentress County, State of Tennessee.* Tennessee Department of the American Legion Auxiliary, 1935.

Soland, Lisa. *Sergeant York: The Play.* Nashville, TN: All Original Play Publishing, 2018.

Stallings, Laurence. *The Doughboys: The Story of the AEF, 1917–1918.* New York: Harper & Row, 1963.

Stringer, Harry R. *Heroes All! A Compendium of the Names and Official Citations of the Soldiers and Citizens of the United States and of her Allies who were Decorated by the American Government for Exceptional Heroism and Conspicuous Service Above and Beyond the Call of Duty in the War with Germany, 1917–1919.* Washington, DC: Fassett Publishing Co., 1919.

Sweeney, Daniel J. *History of Buffalo and Erie County: 1914–1919.* Committee of One Hundred, 1920.

Toplin, Robert Brent. *History by Hollywood: The Use and Abuse of the American Past.* Urbana: University of Illinois Press, 2010.

Trout, Steven. *On the Battlefield of Memory: The First World War and American Remembrance, 1919–1941,* Tuscaloosa: University of Alabama Press, 2010.

Turner, Sandra. *Sergeant Alvin C. York: The Making of a Hero and Legend.* CreateSpace Independent Publishing Platform, 2015.

Wecter, Dixon. *The Hero in America: A Chronicle of Hero Worship.* New York: Charles Scribner's Sons, 1941.

York, Alvin C. *Sergeant York: His Own Life Story and War Diary.* edited by Tom Skeyhill. Garden City, NY: Doubleday, Doran, 1928.

German Documents

1st Battalion Operations Report, 23 September 1918—18 October 1918. *Hauptstaatsarchiv Stuttgart. M411 385/2715.*

Gieraths, Guenther. *History of Reserve Infantry Regiment 210.* Druck und Verlag von Gerhard Stalling Oldenburg i. D. / Berlin, 1928.

2. Landwehr Division Diary and Annexes 1.10.18—18.10.18. Folder II 864–33.5.

Record Group 165. National Archives and Records Administration, College Park, MD.

Lieutenant Thoma 7th Bavarian Mineur Company Statement of 11 October 1919. *Bayerische Hauptstaatsarchiv. Abteilung IV Kriegsarchiv. Muenchen. Personal Akten von Lt. Thoma. OP 14800*

Strom, Gustav. *The Wuerttemberg Landwehr Infantry Regiment Nr. 120 in the World War 1914—1918.* Verlagsbuchhandlung, Stuttgart 1922.

War Diary of 2nd Battalion, Landwehr Infantry Regiment Nr. 120 from 1 June, 1917 to 4 December 1918. *Hauptstaatsarchiv Stuttgart. M411 386/2723.*

War Diary of the 1st Machine Gun Company, 120th Landwehr Infantry—1 October 1918—6 December 1918. *Hauptstaatsarchiv Stuttgart. M411 388a/ 1389*

War Diary of the 3rd Battalion, Landwehr Infantry Regiment 120 From 1 July 1918 to 4 December 1918. *Hauptstaatsarchiv Stuttgart. M411 388/2733.*

War Diary of the Regimental Staff from the Landwehr Infantry Regiment 120 From 1 July 1918 to 1 December 1918. *Hauptstaatsarchiv Stuttgart. M411 382/2700.*

Government Documents

Danaher, Senator John A. *The exploit of Bernard Early at Chatel-Chéhéry.* Congressional Record, 77 (August 7, 1941): S 6864.

"Headquarters 164th Infantry Brigade." General Orders No. 1. May 4, 1919.

House Bill. House of Representatives. *Authorizing the President of the United States to appoint Corp. Bernard Early as a major in the United States Army and then place him on the retired list.* HR 8420, 75th Cong., 2nd sess., introduced in House November 17, 1937.

House Bill. House of Representatives. *To allow the Distinguished Service cross for Service in the World War to be awarded to Otis B. Merrithew.* HR 7340, 71st Cong., 2nd sess., introduced in House, December 11, 1929.

House of Representatives. *H.R. 10297.* 67th Cong. April 7, 1922.

HR 864. 72nd Cong., 1st sess., introduced in House, December 8, 1931.

HR 2427. 73rd Cong. 1st sess., introduced in House, March 9, 1933.

McKellar, Senator Kenneth D. *Promotion of Alvin C. York to the Rank of Colonel. Congressional Record,* 77. S 6411. July 29, 1941.

"Medal of Honor for Bernard Early Resolution." American Legion Department of Connecticut, August 10, 1935.

The National Archives at College Park. College Park, Maryland. Record Group Title: *Records of the Office of the Quartermaster General, 1774–1985.* Record Group Number: *92.* Roll or Box Number: *589.*

Propaganda in Motion Pictures: Hearings before a Senate Subcommittee on

Interstate Commerce, United States Senate, 87th Cong., 2nd sess., Washington, DC: Government Printing Office, 1942.

Record Group 92, Burial Files, Records of the Graves Registration Services, NARA College Park, MD.

Records of the Army War College. Thomas File. RG 165. NARA. College Park, MD.

Regimental Special Orders No. 134. November 3, 1918. NARA, St. Louis, MO.

Representative Thomas J. Lane, In Memory of "Paddy" Donohue—a Member of Sergeant York's Famous Squad in World War I. Congressional Record, 87 (February 19, 1962): S 2501.

"Testimony of German Officers and Men about Sergeant York." translated by the US Army War College. Carlisle, PA, June 1936.

U.S. Congress. *Congressional Record*. 87th Cong., 2nd sess., 1962. Vol. 108, pt. 2.

U.S. Congress. *Public Law 104–106 (National Defense Authorization Act)*. S 1124. 104th Cong. February 10, 1996.

War Department. General Orders No. 22. December 31, 1929.

War Department. *Medal of Honor Citation*. General Orders No. 59. May 3, 1919.

"World War I Draft Registration Cards, 1917–1918." World War I Selective Service System Draft Registration Cards, 1917–1918. NARA microfilm publication.

Interviews

Interview with Jimmy Fallon, December 27, 2019.
Interview with Robert D'Angelo, March 15, 2019.
Interview with David Kornacki, March 21, 2019
Interview with Patricia Walters, August 8, 2019.
Interview with Ned Buxton, January 16, 2019.

Manuscript Collections

Alvin C. York. U.S. Army Service Record. National Personnel Record Center, St. Louis, MO.

Bernard Early Documents. Personal Collection of Robert D'Angelo.

Cutti and Merrimana Folders. White House Central File. Lyndon B. Johnson Library, Austin, TX.

Edward M. Kennedy Senate Files. John F. Kennedy Library. Boston, MA.

George Brand Duncan papers, 1882–1948. University of Kentucky Special Collections Research Center.

John J. Pershing Papers. Library of Congress. Washington, DC.

Joseph Kornacki Documents. Personal Collection of David Kornacki.

Otis Merrithew Documents. Personal Collection of Jimmy Fallon.

Sergeant York Files. Warner Bros. Archives. Archives at USC Libraries, USC, Los Angeles, CA.

Newspapers

Albany Times-Union, Albany, NY
Altoona Mirror. Altoona, PA
Arizona Republic. Phoenix, AZ
Belvidere Daily Republican. Belvidere, IL
Boston Herald. Boston, MA
Buffalo Evening News. Buffalo, NY
Chattanooga Daily Times. Chattanooga, TN
Chicago Tribune. Chicago, IL
Corsicana Daily Sun. Corsicana, TX
Daily News. New York
Democrat and Chronicle. Rochester, NY
Eagle Tribune. Lawrence, MA
El Paso Evening Post. El Paso, TX
Evening Public Ledger. Philadelphia, PA
Fort Lauderdale News. Fort Lauderdale, FL
Fort Worth Star-Telegram. Fort Worth, TX
Hartford Courant. Hartford, CT
Hattiesburg American. Hattiesburg, MS
Holyoke Daily Transcript. Holyoke, MA
Independent. Long Beach, CA
Johnson City Press and Staff-News. Johnson City, TN
Journal Gazette. Mattoon, IL
Lubbock Morning Avalanche. Lubbock, TX
Marshfield News-Herald. Marshfield, WI
Nashville Banner. Nashville, TN
New Haven Evening News. New Haven, CT
News-Press. Fort Myers, FL
News-Reporter. Hubbard, OH
New York Herald Tribune. New York, NY
Norwich Bulletin. Norwich, CT
Oakland Tribune. Oakland, CA
Ontario County Journal. Canandaigua, NY
Providence Journal. Providence, RI
Public Opinion, Chambersburg, PA
Seminole Producer. Seminole, OK
Shamokin News-Dispatch. Shamokin, PA

The Springfield Daily Republican. Springfield, MA

The Springfield Union. Springfield, MA

St. Louis Post-Dispatch. St. Louis, MO

Sunday Herald. Bridgeport, CT.

The Albany-Decatur Daily. Albany, AL

The Bee. Danville, VA

The Boston Globe. Boston, MA

The Boston Sunday Globe, Boston, MA

The Bridgeport Post. Bridgeport, CT

The Bristol Herald Courier. Bristol, TN

The Californian. Salinas, CA

The Chattanooga News. Chattanooga, TN

The Coos Bay Times. Marshfield, OR

The Courier-Journal. Louisville, KY

The Daily Chronicle. De Kalb, IL

The Daily Courier. Connellsville, PA

The Daily News-Journal. Murfreesboro, TN

The Daily Times. Salisbury, MD

The Evening Sun. Hanover, PA

The Evening Tribune. Lawrence, MA

The Greenville News. Greenville, SC

The Honolulu Advertiser. Honolulu, HI

The Indiana Gazette. Indiana, PA

The Kane Republican. Kane, PA

The Knoxville Sentinel. Knoxville, TN

The Los Angeles Times. Los Angeles, CA

The Miami News. Miami, FL

The Morning Call. Allentown, PA

The New Haven Evening Register. New Haven, CT

The New York Times. New York City, NY

The North Adams Transcript. North Adams, MA

The Ogden Standard-Examiner. Ogden, UT

The Philadelphia Inquirer. Philadelphia, PA

The Rock Island Argus. East Moline, IL

The St. Joseph News-Press. St. Joseph, MO

The Sunday Republican, Waterbury, CT

The Tampa Times. Tampa, FL

The Tennessean. Nashville, TN

The Town Talk. Alexandria, LA

The Tribune. Coshocton, OH

The Twin-City Daily Sentinel. Winston-Salem, NC

The Vincennes Sun-Commercial. Vincennes, IN
The Washington Times. Washington, DC
The Wellington Daily News. Wellington, KS
The Whitewright Sun. Whitewright, TX
The Windsor Review. Windsor, MO
Wilkes-Barre Times Leader, The Evening News. Wilkes-Barre, PA

Index